Unity In Everything That Is

ENLIGHTENED WARRIORSHIP UNDER THE GUIDANCE OF 13 MASTERS

By Frank Coppieters, Ph.D.

ConsciousLiving.Media

UNITY IN EVERYTHING THAT IS : ENLIGHTENED WARRIORSHIP UNDER 13 MASTERS

For information contact :

Frank Coppieters @ https://livinglightcenter.com

Book and cover design by Aaron C. Yeagle

Book ISBN: 978-1-7333510-0-3

Kindle ISBN: 978-1-7333510-1-0

First Edition: August 2019

10 9 8 7 6 5 4 3 2 1

Dedicated to my beloved teachers.
They planted seeds in me, which keep sprouting.
I carry them all in my heart.
They are who I am. I am who they are.

Gratitudes/ Acknowledgments

FIRST OF ALL, I would like to thank my deceased parents, Jacqueline and Georges. Both of you worked so very hard to provide me and my two brothers with a safe home. Even though there were many times you were afraid of where my path was going, you remained open, curious and were even willing to learn from me. In spite of your extensive war trauma, you were grateful for the gift of life. You are always present in my heart.

Gratitude to my fantastic brothers. As the middle one — a perfect place for a nine in the enneagram — I always found somebody to play with or be with. Rudy, you protected me when needed and encouraged me to forge my own path. I believe your research into our family tree is supported by our ancestors.

Filip! We have been searching together for many lifetimes. Even as young kids we had deep discussions about the mystery of existence itself. Now I fully realize how very unusual this was. Even before I did, you experimented with communal life and told me tales about India and Osho. You caught many errors in the Dutch edition of my book and thereby saved my bacon! Your spiritual name is Gyandip, Lamp of Wisdom, and Osho chose it wisely.

I thank my ancestors, and especially all the male, female and androgynous shamans among you.

I thank my sister-in-law Christina and my goddaughter Sara for our heart connection. You are two wise women of my immediate family and I am always happy when I see you.

Dearest Kathy, you have already stood for 33 years next to me, through amazing love, minor sufferings and lots of joy and laughter. You are my muse and enthusiastic supporter. Thank you for always being there.

Cher! I remember seeing you jumping in the Ganges, without fear. You have been a true "developmental editor" for the English version of my book and a dream come true. You knew which stories I had not yet told and where to put them. You made the hard work easy for me. Our days with you and George in Dunedin, Florida, were filled with light and laughter.

Some of my students/friends shared their homes so I could write in peace: Klara, Greet and Stephan, Sophie, Mark and Regine, Laurence Kluft, Neal Nemhauser. Thanks!

Laurence Verwee — you gave me great ideas for the Dutch edition.

Luc and Lieve — for your dedication and trust in Kathy's and my work.

Jozef van de Venne for collecting the Inspired Guidances and donating the mother drum to Bois-le-Comte.

I acknowledge and thank my big Reiki family, and especially Paul Mitchell for the gift of Reiki I, Phil Morgan for Reiki II and

Mastership, and Phyllis Furumoto: you being the intrepid lineage bearer of Usui Shiki Ryoho.

Francis Lucille, for your mastership, wisdom, hospitality, and love as you transmit the direct path to me and Kathy.

Rose Okada for being my music teacher.

To Helen Schucman, Eileen Dann, Gitta Mallasz, and Ian Graham for the integrity of your channeling and introducing me to the world of sacred spirit guides.

Lloyd Lemmermann for your incredible support as my friend, sound engineer and photographer, and also for the deep respect for my work and that of Jóska.

Monique Franken and Jürgen and Tamara Ingels for spreading Jóska's work after his passing. Birgit Knorr, my dear friend, for allowing me to publish her paintings of Jóska.

Finally, to the many hundreds of students that have crossed my path. What an honor to search and walk together into the mystery of what is.

Just after I finished writing these Gratitudes/Acknowledgments, I got word from JanieAnn that her husband John Snyder had passed away. It was my great honor to initiate John as a Reiki Master in 2009. John was a lover of the Inspired Guidances and was able to quote many passages by heart.

In a tribute to you, dear John, I am sharing here the Guidance that came through for you and JanieAnn, just minutes after your initiation. I will miss you dearly.

Only love matters.
You, who are the lovers of truth,
the lovers of God,
the lovers of All that Is,
the lovers of love,
you are the salt of the earth
and the crystalline structure
that connects earth to the sacred temple of the cosmos.

Initiation is transformation,
is transition to a higher state
where the divine can use you
as a finely tuned instrument
for her work to allow love to reign
as the supreme reality.

Today you are most welcome in her shrine.
You are dedicating to serve her forever
and through this you become empowered.

You have heard the call since you were young.
You have searched and searched.
Here you are, in the eternal Now,
where there is peace, completion,
and a strong, new beginning.

You are so rich.
You are so wise in your innocence.
The masters are blessing you for stepping forward.

What Usui received on the mountain is alive as ever.
It is medicine and miracle
and enters the hearts of everyone it touches.

Contents

Foreword

FRANK COPPIETERS HAS KIND eyes and a big warm smile. When you meet him, you sense that you can totally relax, just be yourself, and be seen in your best light. It's delightful to be with him. And you realize that beneath the welcoming sweet exterior, he generates a powerful magic infused with ancient wisdom.

Whether or not you've met him in person, you will be spending wonderful time with Frank as he shares stories and highlights from the teachings of 13 of the masters who helped him to evolve spiritually. He is a Reiki master, shaman, healer, workshop and retreat leader, and professor of theater and literature, to name a few of his "hats," and bridges everyday living with a knowledge informed by centuries of art and healing.

I first met Frank and his wife Kathy at a retreat, and was drawn to them right away. They embody intelligence, fearlessness, freedom, and joy in life — the antithesis of the conventional and fearful mainstream culture I was raised in. I got the chance to know them much better when I joined a trip they were leading in India. As Kurt Vonnegut Jr. says, "Unexpected travel suggestions are dancing lessons from God," and I long had a wish to go to India, so I signed up. Frank and Kathy's loving, light and steady presence shepherded us through many adventures, including my personal trauma of a painful divorce, puja in a cave high on Mt. Arunachala, dips in the roaring green Ganges in the Himalayan foothills, a bone-jarring bus ride that lasted most of one rainy night, and the unfortunate "Delhi belly" illness that felled about half our group.

We visited many shrines and places of interest, each experience deepened and informed by Frank's knowledge of the related sages and masters who had lived there.

Each morning we met for a meditation and ceremony where Frank spontaneously vocalized the Inspired Guidances (you will find many in this book). Each of these poetic teachings is unique, fitting the place and moment. You will certainly find some favorites here that particularly speak to you. There are those I cherish and read regularly.

I was quite honored that Frank asked me to be the developmental editor for the English version of this book... what a joy to work on! It is like hanging out with Frank. He writes clearly and richly about profound matters, with a gentle sense of humor. I am often touched as I read and re-read the work. Each time something different stands out for me.

Whether or not you are a spiritual seeker, you will have heard of some of these masters. You may be called to discover more about a particular master, or the many other persons, films, and books he references. I found myself following Internet trails to learn more — seeking out videos, articles, and photos that bring these people to life. Sometimes tears came or joy filled me when just looking at some photo on the Internet. Whether you are on the path or curious about it, this book is a treasure of knowledge and possibilities. I especially hope you will partake of the wisdom that Frank has distilled from a lifetime of teachings. This eternal wisdom is also very relevant to our times.

Frank lives from the heart. He is eternally optimistic, but does not bypass evidence of the ignorance, pain and suffering to be found in the world. References to historical and current heart-rending human events are also found in this book. Yet, Frank's life and this book are a testament to *not* drowning in helpless, sad resignation, but living in a clear-eyed way that honors the mystery, humor, kindness, support, healing, and presence that is possible. This teaching reveals the wisdom of listening to and living in accordance with your inner voice, no matter what others in the world think you should be or expect you to do.

Cher Johnson
Developmental Editor

Preface

DO YOU SOMETIMES LIE awake at night, full of worries, wondering how — for heaven's sake — humanity will ever get it right? Often, the pressing planetary problems as well as those in your own life feel like a heavy burden. You are certainly not alone in this. In spite of all the progress made in the world, injustice remains, painful and demoralizing. Many socio-economic structures are falling apart, but they have not been replaced by something better. The concentration of wealth and therefore power intensifies into the hands of fewer people. Even the environment itself is jeopardized to such an extent that it threatens civilization as we know it. It is tempting to believe that an era of destruction and deep loneliness has begun.

It is almost impossible *not* to struggle regularly with these thoughts and feelings. In this book, I intend to sound a message of hope based on what I myself have been privileged to receive — a hope which is based on the reality of my own experiences and the many others who are walking an authentic path. This path is far from easy, and yet it is, in principle, directly accessible to anyone. This I will illustrate and explain — as simply as possible — from different vantage points.

You, my dear reader, have helped me to write this book! This is really the case, though you may be wondering how this could be possible.

I have tried to listen, as shamans have done for hundreds of thousands of years, to what the earth needs and what you, who are living here now, desperately need. What kind of information is inspiring and useful and practical enough to set something in you into motion? With this question in my heart, I have written this book. I wrote it also for myself, to see even more clearly the threads existence itself has already woven for me. My gratitude towards you, my guides and my teachers, is enormous. Some of you I have known for a very long time. Others are still new to me. Many are sitting next to me as an invisible and strong presence while I am writing.

The first guide I would like to introduce you to, for a moment, is Papa Legba, an ancestral storyteller from the African tradition. He is sitting at the crossroads of space and time, where he is spinning worlds into perception with words and symbols. He carries the key with which to open your heart, and he invites you to remember that everything and everyone is connected to one another. He is asking you, *"Is the story you are currently telling yourself one that pushes you forward, or one that takes you down?"* He counsels you to use words of power for yourself and for others. It is possible to meet in your heart a wise grandfather or grandmother. You could call him or her your inner teacher or master. Or you can think of them as "intuition."

Papa Legba is not that well-known in the West. I met him first in the beautiful *Rainbow Earth Tarot* deck made by an honored friend of mine from Jamaica. There are literally thousands of guides and angels who make themselves available to humanity. In Buddhism, for example, Avalokiteshvara is the most beloved of bodhisattvas. A bodhisattva is considered to be a being who refrains from entering nirvana in order to help others in their process of awakening.

Avalokiteshvara is portrayed in different cultures as male or female. He/she is often depicted with two, or four, or forty-eight, or even a thousand arms! In China or Tibet, we can see him/her as Kuan Yin or Chenrezig, and in Japan as Kannon or Kanzeon. Mostly (s)he stands for compassion and healing. Did you know that many people consider the current Dalai Lama as a manifestation of Avalokiteshvara? As recently as May 27, 2017, he was giving Avalokiteshvara initiations at the Main Tibetan Temple in Dharamsala, India.

For many years now, I have been in touch with miraculous beings of light and love who have words of inspiration for myself and others. The time has come for me to share this with a larger audience than before. I will tell my own story of how this came to pass, and of my unending gratitude.

In Part I, I share some key moments in my life, including my near-death experience at age four, and the dramatic events (at least for me) which created an opening to the guides and angels.

Part II gives you seven simple keys to help you find your way around the spiritual path. I quote from collected works of *Inspired Guidance*... the "voice" which addresses me, and now also you. Later I will relate how the *Inspired Guidances* began during a 1991 session with a medium in London, when I promised to publicly share these words of wisdom that I receive.

In Part III I present you with 13 masters with whom I have established some form of intimate contact. Eventually, they will take you to several manifestations of the divine mother, who was already being worshipped in ancient times as the animating force of the universe. At the end of each chapter I include some of the masters' insights (in my own words or theirs) which have most helped me on my path. Then I share one or more *Guidances* from the many hundreds that I have been receiving almost daily since the year 2000. The ones selected evoke the ideas or the essence of that master. All the *Guidances* are addressed to the heart.

You will find that these masters, each in their own way, are noble warriors fighting for a better world. They are not driven by fanaticism and certainly not by self-importance. They see and experience the unity in everything that is. This they want to share, since they have realized what they are, and they know that you are this as well. Hence the title of this book: *Unity in Everything That Is.*

I call their warriorship "enlightening" because one can find here a multiplicity of meanings. For example:

- Through their presence and actions, they lighten and relieve the pain in the world.
- Their enlightened consciousness is a very direct mirroring of the pure light which is present in the cosmos and in the consciousness of all beings. Also in you, also in me.
- To worship these masters as entities outside of us does not make sense — that would create separation yet again. Instead, see them as illuminating examples.
- In numerology, the number 13 is considered to be the number of the master. Sometimes the reference points very specifically to Jesus and his 12 disciples. You will see that I have a soft spot for Jesus. Not the Christ of my youth nailed to the cross, but rather Jesus as a Zen teacher and older brother from whom we can learn. All the masters in this book are manifestations of the one, the unnamable, the indivisible.

In Part IV I address you always, dear reader, as a beacon of light. Maybe this will take getting used to, but I can promise you the following: even though inner work to get rid of old conditionings has to be done, the light inside of you can recognize immediately and directly what is true. Even if your regular mind can't always grasp this, your heart already knows it. Part IV mostly speaks for itself.

Here I have divided the *Meditations* or *Inspired Guidances* into three chapters, each one with a short introduction. Dear reader, please allow yourself to be taken home in each meditation. You can start or finish your day with one of them; you can read them to your loved ones. Notice that they will work on you both consciously and unconsciously. You can also open yourself to receive your own *guidances*.

Part 1. Key Events

1953

I am just shy of turning four years old when I receive an initiation into the mystery of existence. My mother is the first one to realize that something is very amiss with me, and it could very well become fatal...

The family doctor makes the wise decision to hospitalize me right away. I am extremely dehydrated and in a state of anaphylactic shock. There I am, hovering between life and death for a day and a half.

I am very cold lying in the emergency room. I hear the voice of a doctor telling me how brave I am, as he gives me one injection after another. My family doctor is also present, and his touch is warm and reassuring. His name, in Dutch, is "The Bear" and his aura of strength and protection enters me.

I feel very vulnerable yet strangely unafraid. I see wondrous worlds of light and love. Much later I will realize I am having my first out-of-body experience. Especially the figure of Mother Mary stands out. She looks at me with incredible kindness. I have some thoughts that maybe I did something wrong for this to be happening. She laughs at such silly thoughts.

I know that my grandmothers, in "real" life, are praying for me. I can feel that my parents and my older brother love me a lot.

Unity In Everything That Is

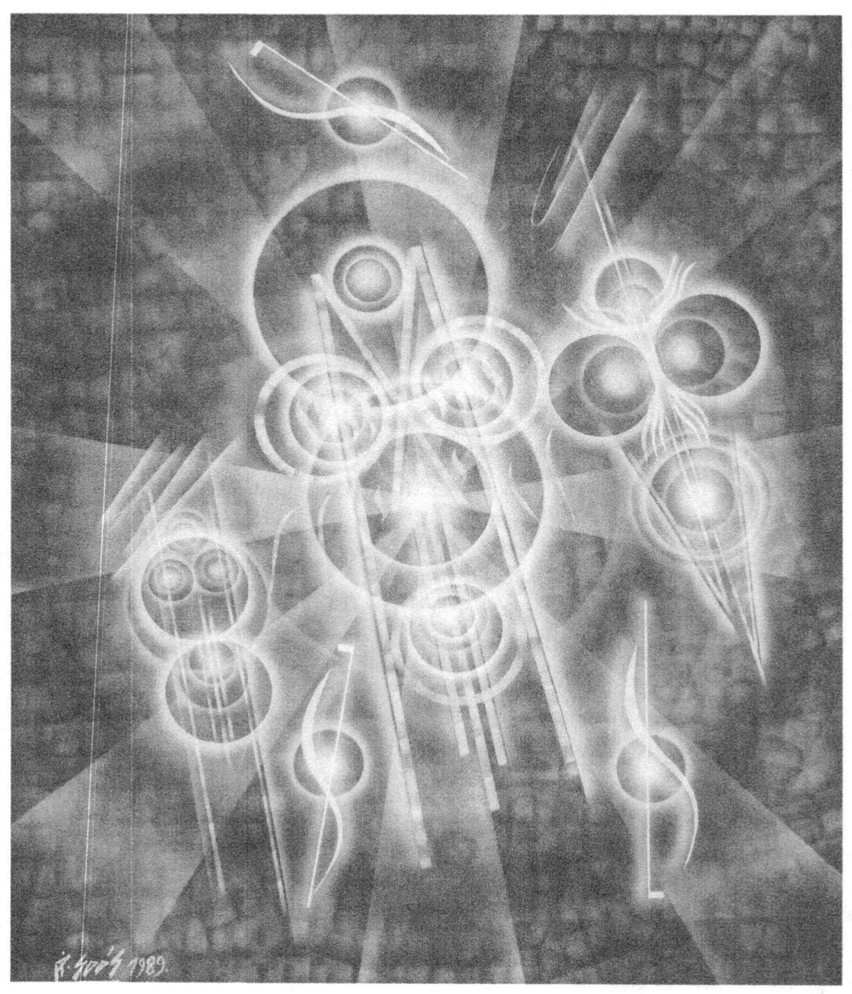

Even my younger brother, who is still a baby, seems to be aware of what is going on and helping. I know that I will remain with my family on earth. This I know for certain. I am aware that the grownups are not sure of this but are doing their utmost to keep me here. For this I am grateful.

Naturally I have the consciousness of a child. I know that it is better not to talk about what I have experienced. Also, I don't know how to. Even now I do not. Except that now I am very certain that this experience gave a particular direction to the rest of my life. Later, in my professional life, it turns out this had been a good preparation to go in and out of body at will, on behalf of people who need healing or transformational work.

1960

I am now ten years old, acting on stage in a small theatre in my hometown of Ghent, Belgium. Many people come to see the play, *Dr. Korczak and the Children*, a moving story about events that took place during the Holocaust. The lead actor and the director are famous in Flanders.

How did I get involved in this avant-garde theatre production?

Now it is my privilege to introduce my father onto the "stage." He was a rather shy and self-effacing man, and also an excellent grade school teacher. He wanted to encourage a special quality he observed in me, so arranged for me to take classes in speech and declamation after school. When the theatre world contacted his school to look for a boy who could hold his ground in public performances, he encouraged me to audition.

The central character of this docudrama is Dr. Janusz Korczak, a Polish Jew, neurologist and reformer in pedagogy. He himself lost his father at a very young age and worked in an orphanage where he formed a close bond with its more than sixty children. They say that he lived a life of love and never lied. Except once. At the end of his life he made the conscious choice to sacrifice his opportunity for freedom so he could accompany his children to a camp (Treblinka) where they will be gassed. As he walks with them through the streets of Warsaw he lies to them and says that their journey to the promised land has started...

During the long rehearsals that stretch late into the night, I am the only child in a world of adults. I cannot grasp a lot of the discussions, but they intrigue me. The play tries to find sense and ethics in the midst of the madness of the Holocaust. I start to think about good and evil. I learn how to empathize. In the play, I embody two different roles: Jürgen, the son of a German officer, and David, a Jewish orphan.

Just as in my home, the actors talk a lot about the atrocities of the war. Belgium had been under German occupation during the war and many wounds were not yet fully healed. I know that my father had been part of the resistance movement, and I am secretly quite proud of this. I consider him my hero.

I remember that I get goose bumps when the name "Jahweh" is uttered on stage, even though I have no clue what this name means.

The newspapers publish rave reviews about this somber avant-garde play and its ethical questions. As a token of honor towards Dr. Korczak, the actors ask the audience not to applaud at the end of the performance. The silence at the end is profound and deafening.

I make a scrapbook of the performance with pictures and clippings from the reviews. In moments of self-doubt or during attacks of low self-esteem as a teenager, I will read these reviews to myself. Especially the one printed in the socialist newspaper of my home town... "No one will hold it against me that I am giving some special praise to Frank Coppieters, as the child. This dapper boy was a complete match for this difficult task."

All these memories resurface in full force when I am in Israel for the first time in 2009 with a group of my students. We are visiting Jerusalem: the area of Qumran (where the Dead Sea Scrolls were found), the West Bank, and also the Holocaust Museum, where there is a big square with a beautiful statue of Dr. Korczak and his children.

In 2017 I am watching the movie *The Zookeeper's Wife*. It tells the account of the keepers of the Warsaw Zoo, Antonina and Jan Zabinski, who helped save hundreds of Jews during the Nazi occupation. Dr. Korczak is portrayed several times, including the journey with his kids to the "promised land."

Later in my life, through the workshops I teach and the meditations I offer, the possibility of peace and harmony in a world in chaos will always be present.

1962

It is the day of my confirmation in the Catholic Church. When I receive the touch on my cheek from the bishop, it leaves an energetic imprint for many years to come — hard to define and at the same time, very palpable. Much later I understood that I had passed through a portal of initiation.

The feast my parents organized was certainly very nice, but that whole day my real interest is somewhere else. I am reading a serious story and again, it has a Jewish frame of reference. It deals with a boy named "Tanguy" and it takes place in a concentration camp. I cannot put it down, even while we are eating our meal.

Several times I am chided for this, but it is impossible to budge me. This was atypical behavior for me. In retrospect, I know that I was partly in another dimension. This will happen more often from now on. At some point this will even become an aspect of my profession. One part of my consciousness is fully present in the here and now. As the same time, I find myself in another reality, which feels even more real.

Later I will read about this in *The Little Prince* when the desert fox is sharing his secret with the prince. "Goodbye," says the fox. "And now here's my secret, a very simple secret: It is only with the heart that one can see rightly; what is essential is invisible to the eye."

"What is essential is invisible to the eye," repeats the little prince, so he can remember it well.

March 1969 - January 1973

I am working on my Master's degree in Literature and Linguistics at Ghent University, Belgium, and for weeks on end the majority of the students, myself included, are "occupying" the lecture halls on the campus. The student revolt of Paris and Berkeley has reached my home town. Students everywhere are fed up with capitalism and consumerism and American imperialism. In France today, "May '68" is still remembered as a cultural, social and moral turning point.

I have nonstop discussions with my fellow students, and also with my parents. I am outraged by the outdated and irrelevant topics and methods most professors are using. I feel the winds of change that characterize the sixties. Five of us decide to teach ourselves the class on theatre performance. It is a big success. We each teach a lecture in place of the drama professor, who was incompetent and should never have received this job in the first place. The other students love the quality of our material and interactions with the audience, and attend in large numbers.

I am constantly agonizing about my own destiny and purpose, but cannot seem to find it. The searching, the idealism and the inspiration of those times will always stay with me.

I write my master's thesis on the renowned British playwright Arnold Wesker. Together with John Osborne, he is one of the so-called *Angry Young Men*. He becomes very well-known with his play *The Kitchen*, which is a hit in both the West End in London and on Broadway in New York. After reading a collection of his essays, *Fears of Fragmentation*, I decide to research his Centre 42 movement, an effort to involve working class populations in the arts with the help of the trade unions.

Arnold Wesker grants me an interview. I travel to London and he cooks me a great brunch in his own kitchen! Later he will become very enthusiastic about my thesis. He writes me a post-card encouraging me to get it published by the British publishing house Hodder & Stoughton. I am very flattered.

Because of my academic grades and the success of my thesis, I am offered a teaching job immediately after graduating. My father is furious when I refuse this. He is deaf to my argument that the professor who would be my Ph.D. adviser is exactly the same one whose classes we taught during the rebellion, because we considered him underqualified.

Instead I participate — with no pay — in a three-month avant-garde theatre project under the guidance of Nijo, my best friend from college. He has studied with the Polish director Jerzy Grotowski, and every day we work long hours using his methods of improvisation: we do voice exercises; we explore the Alexander technique (movement training). At the same time, I am being initiated in Transcendental Meditation (TM). The work with my body and the daily meditation practice have a profound impact on me. A new world opens for me.

On January 1,1973, I acquire a position as an assistant professor in the new graduate program at the University of Antwerp. This immediately begins a period of joyful, dynamic enterprise for me. My liberal department offers almost unlimited possibilities and academic freedom. And, my parents are very happy that their son is realizing his and their dreams.

1975

I am preparing my Ph.D. thesis and receive a grant to study for three months in Paris under the guidance of Roland Barthes (1915-1980). I cannot believe my good luck. He is a famous figure in France and abroad. Susan Sontag rightly predicted that of all the intellectual notables who have emerged in France after the war, his work would certainly endure. And by now (2018) we know it has. He is a key figure in the structuralist approach to literature and language, a philosophy that strives to uncover the implicit and often unnoticed structures that underlie human activity and history.

All the intellectuals in France know Roland Barthes. He is in the same formidable group as Foucault, Lacan, and Claude Lévi-Strauss.

I am entitled to participate in his intimate seminars, and we discuss my work while having coffee somewhere in the Quartier Latin. I feel quite inarticulate in his presence — my French is okay but not great. But he turns out to be very gentlemanly; he gives me his undivided attention and supports the direction and shape of my academic research.

Much later I will realize the full scope of what I learned from being near him and studying his writings. All of them encourage the reader to think outside the box of received opinion. He compares, for instance, how the ideologies which seek to dominate our lives will try to devaluate both sex itself and the pleasure and love it can give us: Marxism seeing sex as a distraction from the class struggle, Christianity seeing the love of human beings as a pale form compared to the love of God, and Freudianism focusing endlessly on all the problems involved in sexuality. Barthes lives in me as a philosopher/anthropologist and critical interpreter of the myths of daily life and popular culture.

These three months in Paris awaken my sensitivity and appreciation for language and art. I see that the use of language is not innocent at all. Language can connect or separate. I am being prepared for a future task: to find a way to express the inexpressible and to help my students to see for themselves what is true.

1978 -1979

I find a beautiful and spacious loft in SoHo in Manhattan, before the neighborhood becomes fashionable. My roommate, Robert Crowl, is an accomplished painter and charges me $200 rent per month. We are living on the top floor of Ali's Alley, a popular and influential jazz club, and the one drawback is how noisy it gets during the weekend. The owner, Rashid Ali, enjoys chatting with me when he is sitting in the street smoking a joint. He is a spirited jazz drummer best known for playing with John Coltrane.

Once again, I am very lucky. This time I obtain a grant from the ACLS, the American Council of Learned Societies, the leading private institution supporting scholars in the humanities. My self-chosen assignment is to see as many avant-garde theatre performances as possible. Officially I am a scholar in residence at New York University. The director of my studies is Richard Schechner, director of *Dionysus in 69*, editor of *The Drama Review,* founder of The Performance Group and professor at NYU. At that time, he is preparing *The Balcony,* by Jean Genet. Together with the anthropologist Alex Alland, I get to sit through months of very exciting improvisations. I become close with all the members of the cast and I am there when The Wooster Group, an experimental theatre company that has launched the career of many actors, emerges out of The Performance Group. I see Willem Dafoe almost every day and will coach him a bit in Dutch, my own mother tongue, for a Hollywood audition. He gets the part as a Dutch immigrant in his first film role, Michael Cimino's *Heaven's Gate.*

Within a few weeks I feel at ease in Manhattan. I love hearing all the languages from different world cultures around me. Being in this melting pot satisfies an aspect of my soul. The art scene, particularly at this time, is full of innovation. The academic teachings in the theatre and the arts departments are never stuffy, and the people are very open and generous towards me. Richard Schechner invites me to Thanksgiving dinner in his home.

I make many friends during this period, and when I return to Belgium, I will invite them to my campus for workshops and performances: Spalding Gray, Carol Martin, Saskia Noordhoek Hegt, Richard Schechner, Jacques Chwat.

March 15, 1985

I arrive at JFK and show my immigration papers. Two Immigration and Naturalization Service (INS) officers are looking through them.

At that time, I was an official disciple of Osho, an Indian spiritual teacher, and so was my American wife, Kathy Melcher. We had just been married in the little town in Belgium where my parents lived. This was potentially tricky. INS was known for trying to catch Osho followers who use fake marriages as a way to stay in the US. I did not want to raise suspicions and had sent my Osho books and clothes ahead of me to friends in New York.

I feel good about my dossier. I have letters of recommendation from New York University with me. The officers are looking carefully through everything I brought with me and then...

I see a whole plane-load of German Osho followers, in their bright orange garb, coming near the immigration office where I am being questioned. It is obvious they are on their way to the big Spring festival in Oregon, just like me! I am afraid one of them will recognize me, and wave to me.

A conversation ensues between the two officers. The senior officer says to the younger one, “Spring is here; the Rajneeshees have arrived.” The younger does not understand what he’s driving at. The first one explains “Don’t you know about this? They are followers of that Indian guy who has a community in Oregon.”

"How long are they here for?" asks the other.

"My God," he says, "you don't know much, do you... a lot of them never leave."

At that very moment he stamps my temporary visa while my application for a Green Card is being processed. I quickly scurry away. I still live in Oregon with my beloved Kathy...

In 2010 I will finally become a U.S. Citizen. The day I am sworn in at the Court House in Portland, I am one of about fifty, and the only Caucasian that day. Most new citizens had come from Asia, especially India, with many members of their families accompanying them. I am surprisingly moved by the beautiful and heartfelt welcoming speech on videotape by Barack Obama. Many people are crying. Since 9/11 it has become more and more difficult for people to enter and it takes longer and longer to become a citizen. A few years later, immigration issues will become even more tangled.

September 1991

I am spending the weekend with Kathy in Astoria, a quaint and beautiful little coastal town in Oregon. My current reading is *The Urantia Book* (1955). It is a long and remarkable book that came into being through channeled information, with fascinating information on shamanism, on the hierarchies of angels, and a very detailed account of the life of Jesus.

On Friday evening, we are in a restaurant overlooking the ocean, waiting for our dinner to arrive. As I watch the light refractions playing on the surface of the waves, I suddenly have the odd feeling that I have left the physical boundaries of my body. This was not my first such experience. In my chapter on Osho I will share the very first time this happened to me.

I ask Kathy that we not wait for our food, but return to our apartment. In the safety of our own place I am able to fully surrender to the process. I find myself in a very special and refined state of consciousness where I am receiving information. I am "told" that when we drive back to Portland, with Kathy behind the wheel, I should read aloud to her from *The Urantia Book*. "By chance" I read her the passage about Paul, then still called Saul, on his way to Damascus, being struck and blinded by a light from heaven. I was curious why *the voice* insisted on me reading from the *Urantia* book. The relevance becomes clear a month later.

October 1991

I am in London now for a session with Eileen Dann, a respected medium of great integrity, who has been receiving messages while in trance. She does not know me at all. This session will have a huge and lasting impact on me — even to this day!

She is giving me information about a life in the time of Jesus in Palestine where I had a close connection with both Paul and Joseph of Arimathea, for whom I (supposedly) had been some sort of shamanic teacher. I am incredibly and inexplicably moved when I hear this. When she first mentions Paul, I feel shivers. As she talks about Joseph my heart starts beating very fast.

Frankly, I had no idea who this Joseph was, and certainly not that he was the uncle of Jesus and a well-known historical figure at the time. I hear that I was then older than Joseph, and that he adhered to a more conservative ideology and was a strict follower of the Tora. And that he took a great interest in my "out of body" experiences and my knowledge of Greek mythology.

After this remarkable meeting, I find myself for a few days in a multidimensional atmosphere. As a result of the reading, I travel to Glastonbury in England. It is known as the heart of Avalon, the island of the Arthurian legend, and in the local bookshops I find surprising historical material about the presence there of Joseph of Arimathea. On his travels from Palestine to England as a tin merchant, he took his young nephew Jesus with him.

William Blake would write a beautiful poem about this called "Jerusalem." It starts like this:

And did those feet in ancient time
Walk upon England's mountains green?
And was the holy Lamb of God
On England's pleasant pastures seen?

During the session with Eileen in London, "Joseph" asks to transmit messages through me, and I make a solemn promise that I will do my best. Fragments of this session later find their way into the book *The Way of Love: Joseph of Arimathea tells the True Story behind the Message of Jesus* (Peter Wheeler, 1996).

Upon my return to the United States — after long meditations, day after day, for many months — I open myself to receive *words of wisdom*. The process starts in earnest after a visit to Mount Shasta, California, as I begin to record the sessions to capture the precise wording.

September 11, 2001

After the terrible shock of this infamous day, I decide to share the guided messages outside of my limited circle. I felt a bit awkward, shy and insecure about being a medium from some astral dimension. Now I give in to an inner prompting to more actively assist in creating a field of light and love.

In the next couple of weeks, whenever I receive some *Inspired Guidances,* as I have started to call them, I send them to a few dozen friends and students. They are received with great enthusiasm and forwarded to others. My mailing list grows every week. At the request of a student in Belgium, I also translate them into Dutch.

2006

My first book, *Handbook for the Evolving Heart,* is published. Readers respond on a deep soul level. As a result, many more people are requesting to be put on the mailing list. My friend Shama and I collaborate and produce the CD *I Am Calling You,* in which Inspired Guidance meets devotional chant...

2008

My parents in Belgium are aging and my shamanic teacher Jóska Soós has died. Kathy and I decide to start offering more intensive shamanic trainings in Belgium. We go back and forth three times a year to accomplish this. The first group of students who signs up for our "two-year training" refuses to quit, and we are still working with them!

In every single workshop, before breakfast I begin with an Inspired Guidance meditation. Then Kathy and I go around and give a short Reiki blessing to everyone. The tone for the rest of the day is set.

2010

I write the *Credo of the Shaman* ~~

As a shaman I want to clear a path
for the future generations
and allow the wisdom of the ancestors to guide me.

As a shaman I am able to listen to the sounds
of the earth, the stars and the galaxies.
I am able to morph into any form I want
if my intent comes from sacred respect.

As a shaman I weep for the earth
who is being raped and abused
and denied her right to speak for herself.

As a shaman I want to restore the harmony
between all the kingdoms
and be at one

with all the living and the disembodied teachers
of this realm and of all realms
that lovingly interact with us.

As a shaman I want to bring joy
wherever I may sing, celebrate, inspire, awaken.

As a shaman I want to meditate in silence
till the end of time and be the peace
I so strongly want to share with all beings.

As a shaman I am not limited in time, space,
belief, language, culture, history, form.
I Am "That"!

2016

I publish the Dutch version of *Unity in Everything That Is* in Belgium.

2017

With the help of Reiki Home International, I broadcast *Inspired Guidance* live from my home via the Internet. People from many parts of the world are tuning in.

Part 2. Keys

CHAPTER 1

There are no mistakes on your life path

WHO HAS CREATED THE script of my life? When I look at the course of all the events, there is nothing I would change. Also, and least of all, the difficult and painful aspects. In all honesty, it took a very long time before I was truly able to see it like that.

Maybe this is what the spiritual path is all about... a process of becoming conscious and grateful for what there is.

Is it really true that there are no mistakes possible on our life path?

In any case, it is a fundamental leap in consciousness when we are able to look at our life path in this manner, and especially to experience it as such.

We have to make a distinction here about how we deal with things which are obviously going awry. That is, if we can help it. It is not wise, for example, to invest money in ventures which are going bankrupt, to choose a partner who later turns out to be very dysfunctional, to neglect our health to the point of serious illness, to select the *wrong* education or career options, etcetera, etcetera. Sometimes we may not be able to avoid choosing poorly. But everything, literally everything, does belong to the life path. Once we see and understand that clearly and are able to come to terms with it, there is a dramatic change.

From this awakened perspective, we look at everything differently. We are more present in the now since no energy gets lost in regret or guilt. We have more trust in ourselves and in the future because we know that everything can be a help on the path, even each *misstep*. We are less upset and fearful.

Of course, it is never the intent to make mistakes on purpose, and certainly not the same mistakes. We always allow for a learning process. All this is part of openness. Open spirit, open body, open heart.

We are also *miracle-minded*. This does not have to be a woolly new age concept.

I will explain. In physics, it has long been known that everything is interconnected, and that the whole universe has an open quality. Our existence is nested in a web of relationships. In an open system, there is an active readiness to allow for the creation of new possibilities. Miracles are the spontaneous result of this. When you are with people who are open, you simply feel how everything is flowing. When you are together in silence with such a group, it is much easier to stop hectic thinking for a while, and then new ideas and insights can come in.

CHAPTER 2

Linear time does not exist

DEAR READER, FOR ME it is special to connect with you now, as I am writing this. On a certain day you will read these words. We are already connected with one another.

You do know that time does not really exist, right? If you have never heard of this, now is the time!

What do I actually mean by this? The only moment that really exists is now... for instance, this moment while you are reading these words. All other moments are already in the past or are yet to happen in the near or distant future.

Maybe you are thinking that we are splitting hairs here?

Far from it.

This insight, experienced regularly as a reality, very soon becomes the most supreme insight.

Truly!!

I explain further...

Do you not often have the feeling that you are in some sort of a trance state? You are driving to work, and on your way you are thinking of a great many things. Then all of a sudden you have arrived, after a series of multiple moments, all of them succeeding each other.

In a way, you were not really present. It just looked as if you were. This changes very dramatically if you almost or fully have an accident; then all of a sudden you are super alert. Time, as it were, is standing still. Later you can remember everything vividly, precisely because you were so very present.

Do you realize that it is possible to always be present and alert? But in a calm and relaxed way. Effortlessly. Then life — for we are discussing your life in particular — becomes very exciting indeed. Fortunately, without the need for much drama.

Having the courage to be open to the idea that linear time does not exist often leads us into the miraculous world of synchronicity.

When I started to delve into shamanism, I began by reading the classics, such as *Shamanism* and *The Myth of the Eternal Return*, by Mircea Eliade (1907–1986), philosopher and professor of comparative religion. His scholarly works are still worth reading. He tells, for instance, that when a child is born to the Osage Indians, they will first call a shaman who sings about the birth of the world.

The native people take good care when they are telling their myths and performing their rituals, so that one becomes situated in a meaningful world. The emphasis is not so much on linear time — through which time is measured by change — but on cyclic time. In this way, people can live in connection with a primal time, which is bursting with life energy and always repeating itself in the now.

I will never forget how, in a Grotowski project in Poland (*see Chapter 5*), I could participate in a ritual without words with a family from Haiti who had never before left their home country. Every single morning and evening, they connected themselves with the sun for more than an hour. Their total presence and relaxation during these times was out of this world. No hurry whatsoever. As Mircea Eliade would express it, "a real ritual undoes time." Secular time respectfully gives way to sacred time.

As the *Guidance* beautifully puts it:

The real reality, in which everything is divinely connected,
has not changed its essence since time came into being.

« la roue de la reincarnation, via le BARDO-THÖDOL. » J. Gooÿ. 1997

CHAPTER 3

Synchronicity

When I rang the bell of Phil Morgan for the first time, and he opened his door, it was as if he had been waiting there for me for many years. I had never met him before. My friend Joel Saxe had referred me to him as the only professional Reiki practitioner in our town.

When Phil and I looked in each other's eyes, a mutual recognition immediately took place. Later I discovered that Phil is not only a Reiki but also a shamanic practitioner. Just a few years before our meeting, he had given up his career in computers to follow his true path. In 1989 he would initiate me as a Reiki master.

In these first moments, as we look at each other, linear time is not there. Past, present and future are already assembled in those first few seconds.

I know that many people have such experiences when they first meet someone. One could say that in these moments we are multidimensionally present, out of time, and allowing communication to take place at the level of essence.

The rigid laws of time and space release their grip on us for just a little while.

Now I will add that according to the law of synchronicity, time does not really exist.

This law had already been formulated in 1929 by the Swiss psychiatrist Carl Jung. He raised the concept during a visit with Einstein, who immediately responded with great interest. It deals with the phenomenon that certain "accidents" are not accidental at all, at least not in your experience. That is precisely what this is all about. You might experience an event that seems to be an accident, but is also very meaningful.

Most people feel very lost in a universe without meaning. When it turns out that existence is abundant — it signals this to you — this can be either confusing or very liberating. It's confusing when too many signals put you in a hyper-vigilant state, but liberating when you realize that there is never a reason for worry. The solution (to your problem), the way out, the *answer* is already waiting for you exactly where you are.

A friend might say something out of context. Suddenly there is a song about that on the radio. You are switching the television channel and for a second you are struck by the Dalai Lama saying something philosophical. All of a sudden you know — this is it! A light goes on and you make a decision. At these times, you are using existence around you as the *I Ching*, as an oracle.

CHAPTER 4

Gratitude and trust

IN EACH LIFE THERE are turning points. In my own case, I was able to make important life decisions because I had listened with attention to the teachings of the people crossing my path. I trusted that they knew something that I did not yet fully know myself. I am grateful now to myself for having been able to listen, and to them for their willingness to share their wisdom.

For me, a critical moment came when I renounced my princely life as a tenured associate professor at the University of Antwerp at the age of 35. I had taught there for 12 wonderful years. The amount of freedom I had and the license to experiment in my teachings and relationships with my students was truly extraordinary. And yet, the inner *voice* was so compelling that I had to leave this safe haven. There was no escape. I just had to leave. Luckily, I did.

Since then, I have met an unusual number of people, both in my private practice and as a teacher, who are at a critical crossroads in their life. I try to make something clear to them...

If you don't trust that an honorable life path is already laid out for you, you may never find it. You will have to make a jump. If trusting is too difficult, maybe you can commit to being open.

MAAM
" la roue de la reincarnation, via le Bardo-Thödol

Can you, in principle, be open to the idea that there is something in you that has some tiny sense of your life's path?

Do not worry if you are both attracted to and resistant to this idea. Certainly, this was the case for me, and it still bedevils me at times! What we are really talking about here is to experiment, and in this way to find out for yourself what will happen. You will learn how to step through the fear underlying the resistance, and surrender to life. To trust that life itself, and therefore also your life, always has something of great value to offer to you.

Why would existence leave you out or forget about you? Yes, I am talking to you who are reading this right now. Can you see that such a thought only arises when you are in the grip of the past? This type of thought is often connected to an image or feeling of low self-esteem. While believing this thought, you cannot move forward.

Again, and try to be as honest as possible when you answer this — are you willing, if only in principle, to be open to the idea that something in you has a sense of your life path?

Please know that even a little willingness on your part is more than enough to allow a process of opening.

You will see that synchronistic events, masquerading as "chance," will present themselves to take you to your life path. The more alert you are, the better. And never forget this: even a little willingness puts you on the path.

Connected to this is gratitude. When we are grateful, we immediately enter into a higher frequency. It is a vibrational field that relates directly to the continuous stream of abundance, which is present in existence itself.

Gratitude is the perception that the glass is not half empty, but half full. This is not a form of denial or distortion. It is a special moment of choice within the perception itself. An example is when I choose to see myself as gifted, which we truly all are, rather than flawed. When we consciously choose from the place of this perception on a regular basis, we are more and more spontaneously present in life.

Gratitude is a wonderful feeling. I remember how the following meditation dropped into my own heart in 2012. Not coincidentally, it was the day before Thanksgiving. As an immigrant in the U.S., Thanksgiving Day has special significance for me. I still remember the gratitude I felt on being welcomed into the home of Richard Schechner in New York City on Thanksgiving in 1977. He knew I did not have anywhere else to go. Most people there were from the world of theatre, and we shared aloud what we were thankful for in the past year — many very deep sharings.

I was too shy to say much at the time, but I still sense the warm glow of being included in this little family far from home. Manhattan, all of a sudden, felt much less lonely.

Gratitude

Gratitude takes many forms
and each of them has a beauty of its own.

There is the sudden seeing of everything you already have.

There is the deep gratitude for what you already are.

Gratitude for a forefeeling of what you are,
for a sense or a taste of your true origin.

Gratitude for the silence out of which everything arises,
including you.

Gratitude to the saints and sacred beings
in and out of manifestation
who remain committed to your inner development.

Tara de la lumière sonore - safrane de connaissance transcendentale, enseigne

Gratitude to the light that you are and always will be.

Gratitude for your friends and family, biological and spiritual,
for being there for you.

For the spirit animals who love you so dearly.

For the opportunity to partake in evolution
and to propel it forward to a level of dignity.

Gratitude for moving beyond the ego
into the consciousness of oneness.

What is born out of gratitude has a spark of divinity in it
and carries you into infinity.

This moment is filled with bliss
because you are all of this.

peintre-chamaniste-chamanise, 1997/ "BOUDDHA le Haut-Mystique"

CHAPTER 5

You are already perfect

Who is not tormented by a feeling of lack and inadequacy? So often we hear voices in our heads, telling us off. Who would not pay a fortune in order for this struggle to be over? Time and again, as you will see, the *Guidance* is addressing this problem respectfully, with no patronizing.

These *Guidances* honor us in our greatness and encourage us to develop our talents.

What takes place when you are able to say, *I am now perfect just the way I am...?* When you can see that this is true, not just for you but for everyone, the world changes, or at least the way you view and experience your world.

Do you notice how the inner critic starts to mutter and grumble and come up with all sorts of arguments to deny this? Can you see that this is not at all helpful? We are talking here about the essence of your being, and this *must* be good and perfect. Another reason I am deeply grateful for my teachers is that they would repeat this over and over until the truth of it started to trickle through. Drip, drip...

Almost nobody on this planet has parents or even teachers with the ability to see or honor our innate goodness. The results of this are quite horrible. At some point, it becomes just too hard to believe in our own perfection. One job of a real teacher is to offer a new lens, a lens of self-forgiveness through which you can see that everything inside of you is good and perfect as it is. This is true at the level of essence. Of course, in the relative world, there is a place for "work on oneself." Zen sometimes formulates it like this: yes, you are perfect just the way you are and yes, there is still some room for improvement.

Back to forgiveness. Remember what I said about linear time? Forgiveness is nested inside the idea that linear time does not exist. When we are unable or unwilling to forgive, we imprison ourselves in the past, which results in bitterness. Yet I am not saying that we ever have to condone bad deeds or false ideas or destructive ideologies, such as white supremacy or fascism. When I forgive a person, or myself for that matter, it is a conscious choice to shift from the past to the present, which is where I want to be, always.

When we are able to see through the lens of now, we liberate ourselves from old karma. It is true that to some extent we reap what we have sown. But the idea that we have to get rid of all karma — karma in the sense of rubbish from the past — before we are able to see our own perfection, is unnecessarily limiting. It hampers our joy in this moment.

Loving attention

Always keep a sufficient amount of your loving attention
close to yourself.

In this way you will not be needy.
You will not be seeking attention outside of yourself.

As you continue on your spiritual journey
you are bound to discover that your true nature
is in an ongoing state of loving attention, not just for yourself

but for everything that exists.

To the egoic mind believing in lack, this is incomprehensible.
To your open heart it is self-evident.

All authentic spiritual teachings tell you
to trust living from the open heart.
It establishes you in happiness and in the freedom to be what you are.

You can only taste this happiness and this freedom
by experimenting with trusting.

Trusting is innate.
Babies trust.
Regain your innocence by trusting in what you are.

Even before problems arise
a trusting heart has found solutions.

Trusting is not blind.
It is based on a deep resonance with the laws of the universe.

You can certainly trust that an awareness of what you really are
is a great contribution to the well-being of this planet.

CHAPTER 6

The path of joy

THE TWO MOST IMPORTANT insights I received from my teachers are that there is a direct path, and that the essence of my being and that of everyone else is absolutely perfect. I remind myself of this as often as possible (especially when I notice I have "slipped").

From this, it logically follows that we do not have to worry, and certainly not about who or what we are.

And that it is always good for us to allow self-love to be present.

Self-love also means that we can grant ourselves, without begrudging, the freedom to relax in as many situations in our life as possible.

The purpose of life is to be happy — to effortlessly experience true joy. Sometimes even the most evolved spiritual seeker will lose sight of this essential quality. When I introduce Osho (*see Chapter 6)* to you, I will elaborate more on this. He was such a noble bundle of pure joy.

Naturally, in modern life, no one is immune to the hectic tensions all around us. We all know the chronic pain and fatigue that can gather in our body. For this, yoga and body-oriented therapies can be most helpful.

But there is more. What is the basic attitude you entertain toward yourself? How do you talk to yourself? Do you even know? Are you often angry with yourself? Or disappointed in yourself? Has this ever worked? Do you consider yourself to be a (miserable) failure?

Watch out — your joy is in jeopardy.

Even when life is not giving us the quiet we need, we can at least give ourselves the kindness and gentleness we most certainly deserve. When we accept this as a valid insight, we can choose this regularly, and at some point, continuously. Establish a partnership with your innate joy!

The *Inspired Guidances* are, in fact, guided meditations that suggest to the reader again and again to return to a relaxed state of body and mind. If you do not find the time to meditate for a half hour, you can at least do this: take a moment every so often to refresh yourself with a stimulating and true thought. Some examples: *I now choose joy rather than suffering. I choose effortlessness rather than habitual efforting. I choose openness rather than being closed off. I choose self-love rather than self-criticism.* Make room for joy! Right now. You will not regret this.

We have inherited the opinion that there is some profit in worrying or fussing over countless things. That we would be less productive if we were too relaxed. If you have parents that suffered in difficult circumstances, they most likely raised you with such notions of how best to survive.

True, it requires courage to drop limiting thoughts and belief systems. What we "know" often feels safer that what we do not. We are lucky to live in a new era where many people consider "experiencing authentic joy" as a basic human right.

Zest for life arises naturally from a sense of connection. It grants an effortless quality to accomplishing our tasks.

It is not that we want to be passive. We let ourselves listen to the ingenuity and resourcefulness of existence. It sends us to where and with whom we need to be.

From the deep insight that we are naturally good and perfect, we can let go of the tension of searching for a specific method to be or become happy. We let it happen.

How can you give a fresh momentum to your life path? By looking differently at yourself and the world around you. Replace fear with courage. Instead of suffering, choose joy as your teacher.

Path of joy

Always remember —
this time you voluntarily choose the path of joy.

On this path you are a loving friend to yourself.

On this path you enjoy going inside
and finding vast, open space.

On the way, not avoiding anything,
you come upon openness after openness.

Your heart is the guide.
Your open mind is the happy servant.

Such a journey cannot fail.
There is no agenda.
There is no attachment.

States of mind come and go.
Awareness of what you really are
grows, moment by moment.

This awareness is not individual.
It shares itself, simultaneously, with everyone.

This presence, this unobstructed presence,
is not bothered by mind chatter and feelings of inadequacy.
This presence is joy itself, and it is you.

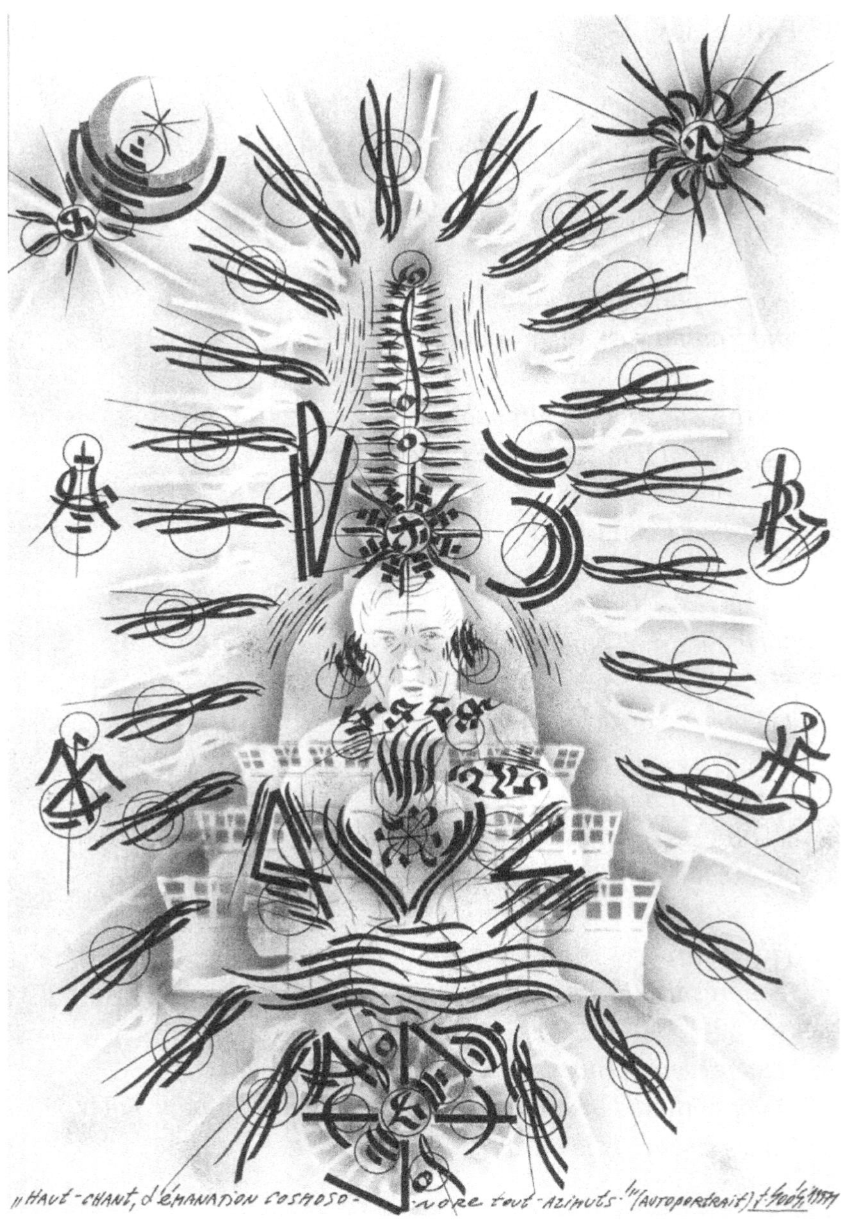
"Haut-chant, d'émanation cosmoso-nore tout-azimuts." (autoportrait)

CHAPTER 7

Dogma and ideology have no virtues

ABDICATE DOGMA IN WHATEVER form it manifests itself.

Please do not to elevate the previous sentence into some new dogma!

Investigate for yourself and find out what works for you.

Trust in the reality of your own experience.

Do not trust or identify with an ideology or belief system.

Certainly not if it turns out to be organized hierarchically.

It will most likely cause you trouble, and it will not make good on its promises.

The tragedy of dogma is that words lose their potency over time. Many beautiful religious texts that came from revelations deteriorate into rigidity. Think of the inspired and loving words of Jesus being misused to treat an opponent with terrible harshness.

The limitation of words is also the frustrating struggle of the mystic. Their experiences come from a very deep and authentic place. They do not doubt the validity and reality of what they saw, and most naturally, are eager to share this with their fellow humans. You have to be creative (like Rumi) to prevent the divine from getting lost in the superficiality of words.

Luckily, creativity exists as a flowing and innovative aspect of the divine. It knows no restraints. Each time a new form of consciousness comes into being, it creates a fresh and open form to express itself. Eckhart Tolle is a perfect example of this.

You may also consider this —

There is no notion conceptualized by thought that is able to give us access to *true* reality. This is most fortunate! Thinking can quickly turn into a means of domination. What is eventually asked from us is to leave all concepts behind. That is the beginning of wisdom...

Whenever possible, establish yourself humbly and innocently in harmony with existence itself. Everyone and everything that transpires within existence is a precious part of it, including you, your life and also all the circumstances of your life.

Some of you may recall the terrible attacks at the Brussels airport in 2016. The day after, while I was still in the United States, I received the following *Guidance*. A few days later I left for three months in Belgium and had frequent opportunities to read it to groups of colleagues and students. Each time, I could feel a very healing frequency descend. In certain circumstances, words can soothe, repair and redirect.

<u>Love</u>

Breathe in love.
Breathe out love.

Now you are in the center of the truth of what you are.

How may humanity ever learn?

The antidote to fear and violence
is listening to what love has to say.

Love has words of wisdom.
Love is the answer and the never-failing comfort.

No event can stop you from reaching for
and finding the peace within you.

United in this, you are bonded
and supported in the oneness of love
and the beauty of your eternal being.

The vastness of your silence is a prayer
and cannot be misunderstood.

It embraces the whole globe
and mitigates the suffering.

You are the light in this world.
Your presence makes a radical difference.

What you are, you share.
Be love.

With every trigger, with every challenge
love renews its invitation
to be what you are.

Part 3. 13 Masters

IN THIS SECTION, I will present you with insights from 13 masters who have left deep imprints on my heart. I asked for inner guidance to decide which of my teachers to include in this book. There could certainly have been more. I also kept in mind what would be of most interest to you. I trust you will be enriched by "meeting" them, as I have been.

Before I introduce you to my selection of masters, I would like to honor my father. In the Dutch language a grade school teacher used to be called a "master."

My father was a grade school teacher. He was an excellent teacher. Everyone would say that about him. He was able to listen, had a lot of patience and was very fair. He was not a grandstander. On the contrary, his main concerns were his pupils and the transmission of knowledge. Quite a few years now since his death, I am still learning from him and always will.

One of his greatest gifts came during the last months he spent on earth. After a stroke in his early nineties, his life had become hard to bear. During one of our visits, Kathy showed him a book of impressionist painters whom he loved. Painting became his hobby after retirement, and we all thought his work was very fine. He looked attentively from one painting to another. Suddenly Kathy asked him, "Hey Georges, is there still any quality of life left for you?" We did not expect an answer, since he had not uttered a single word during our visit. He turned to her, without flinching, and said in impeccable English, "No, and one has to accept that." We were both stunned. There was not a trace of self-pity in this one final sentence I heard from his lips. He was biding his time until my mother gave him her permission to go. When she did, he stopped eating and drinking and in a couple of days made the great leap into the beyond, without any fear. Thank you, Dad!

The first time I saw a picture of the Indian saint **Ramana Maharshi**, an immediate and long-lasting soul recognition took place. He gave me a golden key to the direct path.

The Hungarian shaman and artist **Jóska Soós** did everything possible to transmit to me his connection with the light and sound beings. His clairvoyant and clairaudient perception made it possible for him to interact with these beings from another, sacred dimension. During each of my multiple visits to him, he would encourage me to bring out whatever was still lying dormant in me. When I needed him, he always made himself available, even when he was aging. I am happy that his paintings are *enlightening* this book.

The epic search into the esoteric secrets of healing, by the Japanese Buddhist master **Mikao Usui,** brought me in touch with the art of self-healing.

G.I. Gurdjieff, from Russian Armenia, has been stalking me all of my adult life. His quest for hidden sources of knowledge always fires my imagination. It was under his influence that I experienced the first moments of self-remembering, the remembrance that a real (eternal) self actually exists. He introduced the enneagram to the West, an inspiring symbol of the inner dynamism of the cosmos.

Through practicing with the Polish theatre innovator, **Jerzy Grotowski,** and his colleagues, I learned to listen to and trust the wisdom and creative impulses of my own body.

Osho. For two full years I had the privilege to live in direct physical proximity to this awakened master. He gave me so much, and especially the flame and dance of joy.

The Tibetan lama **Chögyam Trungpa** was a cosmic being. He showed me, by example, that compassion and goodness are innate.

Eckhart Tolle. What a beautiful and radiant representative and emanation of Christ consciousness. I delight in his disarming simplicity, his impish way of making fun of ego.

When my heart had to learn how to be vulnerable, **Jesus** reentered my life. He was no longer the Jesus of my youth but the gnostic Jesus, Jesus as Zen master — Jesus as an older brother showing the way of ongoing forgiveness in the midst of all relationships.

Sri Aurobindo. When India wanted to free itself from the burden of British rule he was viewed as "the most dangerous revolutionary," having studied in England from an early age and mastered English as no other. Later he became the greatest philosopher and yogi of his time, as he developed *integral yoga*.

Mirra Alfassa, better known as **The Mother**. Together with Sri Aurobindo, she is an avatar of human evolution. I constantly feel her as a guide, a protector, a hope for humanity.

When I am in the presence of **Mother Meera,** it is crystal clear that the divine feminine is transforming the consciousness on earth. The new age is here.

Amma, also known as the *hugging saint*, has dedicated her whole life to sharing her immortal bliss and bettering the lives of the downtrodden.

CHAPTER 1.

RAMANA MAHARSHI — The Direct Path

OF ALL TEACHERS, RAMANA Maharshi (1879–1950) moves me the most because of his simplicity, his love, his radiant presence in pure beingness. Once, in a glimpse, I saw that my soul deemed it safe enough to come back to earth because he has been here. I was born about two months after his death in 1950. The first time I saw his picture, I immediately recognized him. I am not the only one who has had this experience — after his life, his silent presence continues to draw truth-seeking humans like a magnet. No one else has made the *direct path* accessible again in such a penetrating and easy fashion.

In 2010, Kathy and I finally arrive in Tiruvannamalai, the town next to the holy mountain Arunachala where Ramana had lived. It had forever been number one on my bucket list. We are there during a full moon, and for this special occasion a million Indian people have gathered. Most have come just for the day, on a never-ending mass of busses. They come to climb or walk around the mountain, and also to pay their respects at Ramana's ashram. They consider him to be a great saint. Lots of children are there, and some incredibly old people too. Almost everyone is barefoot. Mantras are constantly being sung, and the air is filled with ecstatic joy — intoxicating!

We are standing on the road watching this pilgrimage, along with many other spectators. Suddenly two Indian women interrupt their walk as they glance at me and Kathy. We have no idea who they are or where they come from. I feel that they *recognize* us as kindred souls. They have tears in their eyes. We ourselves are also very moved, of course. We greet each other in a *namaste*. They do not speak English. Then they move on, up the mountain, pushed along by the undulating throngs of people.

Ramana was born in 1879 in South India. At the age of 16, he was overcome by a sudden death experience. He was home by himself, and he felt his body becoming cold and stiff. He no longer saw or heard anything. Still, something inside of him was aware of what was going on. Instead of panicking, he made an inner decision to investigate what was happening. In a certain sense — and this is of course very unusual for a boy that age — at that moment he had the presence of mind to accept the situation exactly as it was.

A wordless question arose in him and took the following form: *Who or what is dying here?* As a result, a remarkable change took place. What was apparently dying was his *little self*. It was almost immediately replaced by the emergence of his *real "I"* or *eternal self*. This event would change his life forever.

Shortly afterward, he moved to Arunachala, the holy mountain in South India that is considered to be an emanation of Shiva. He would stay there till the end of his life, fully absorbed in an absolute state of clear and loving presence.

Thousands of spiritual seekers would find their way to him. When they were with him, they could share his silent company for hours, and sometimes there was an opportunity to ask questions. Most of these questions were never answered, at least not in words. Ramana looked at the questioner intently for a long time. When he did say something, he invited the questioner to ask him/herself, *Who am I?* He trusted that this form of self-inquiry was able to let somebody see and experience their true essence.

Ramana's argument and also his method works like this: when you are looking for the I, you suddenly see that it does not really exist. He is referring here to the "I" as an intangible connection between the body and consciousness. In order to survive, the limited "I" (or the little self) has to constantly identify itself with objects such as the body, or concepts such as nationality. In contrast, the real I is not an object, but a subject. It is always present in a self-evident way and is standing completely out of time. It is possible to experience this by going inside and releasing oneself from all false entanglements with objects.

I know from my own experience that it is not always obvious what Ramana is talking about here. Words, after all, have their limitations. However, they can set us on our path. The many meditations in this book serve the same purpose. Again and again, words are used to reference what lies beyond them. Ramana knew this very well. This is why he chose not to talk so often about self-realization. His medium was silence. He felt that true silence was also a conversation.

His silent presence was so palpable that the students had moments during which their identification with the body and the personality suddenly dissolved and catapulted them into limitless freedom and joy.

It is still possible to feel that strong presence in Ramana's ashram, and also around and on Mount Arunachala. Twice, Kathy and I led groups there, and each time that did happen. Everyone experienced deep moments of unity consciousness.

Ramana has become the most well-known representative of the path of insight, also called the *direct path*. He certainly did not intend to proclaim a new religion, but wanted to point to a path that is accessible to anyone. He saw that awareness of this path was only obstructed by the illusory superimposition of a separate mind, a mind separated from the heart.

The path is straight, in that we travel from illusion to knowledge through a proper understanding of the workings of the mind. This implies understanding the mind's nature and its source.

It can be said that Ramana's method was really based on his own death experience. While his body was becoming more and more like a corpse, he asked the question, *Who is dying*? By asking this, there was an immediate upsurge of an "I feeling" separate from the body. Further inquiry revealed that this "I" was more like a force, a center, or a current independent of the body. Later he would always recommend and encourage his visitors to practice this relentless inquiry, a method of diving within, seeking the source of the mind, the source of the I.

Such an inquiry could take the forms of questions such as, *What is aware of your experience? In what are your experiences appearing? From where do your thoughts arise? Is there something present during all your experiences?*

Do not expect verbal answers here. Just stay as open as possible. Chances are that all of a sudden, sometimes during a guided meditation, during a walk in nature, or during a retreat where there is a field of consciousness, you will receive a glimpse. A sincere self-inquiry question triggers the immediate recognition of your essential nature. The direct path has opened for you.

About 70 years after the death of Ramana, this path has become more accessible than ever. The time is right for it, and it is a very hopeful aspect of the evolution of human consciousness — the ability to make a very clear distinction between what is essential and that which is not.

At the core of the direct path is the possibility for everyone to awaken to their true nature. How this occurs will vary greatly.

The most important and deepest insight here is that it makes no sense to postpone this. Tomorrow never comes! There is no time like the present. Why delay?

Paradoxically, the direct path is the invitation to not go anywhere else. You stay with yourself. This path is where you are, not where you are not.

- What is the use of trying to understand the world without first understanding yourself?
- Time is immaterial for the Path of Knowledge.
- Who am I? Not the body, because it is decaying; not the mind, because the brain will decay with the body; not the personality, nor the emotions, for these also will vanish with death.

What are you — really?

What are you — really?
This line of inquiry leads you most directly to Source.

It establishes you in your true identity,
in the timeless, the absolute, the unknowable.

It liberates you from feeling confined in your body,
or in the world for that matter.

What are you really?
The ancient sages and the modern sages asked this question.
Buddha asked it. Jesus did.
Ramana Maharshi suggested it all the time,
to be with this question, to live it.

This question opens you up, both directly and steadily,
to the light within.

The eternal love that greets you here has always been your birthright.

Everything greets you here.
The essence of all that is.

All this you are and more,
from the beginning of time till the end of time.

What Love wants from you is to recognize Her
as your Self.

During the thoughts...

During the thoughts and also in the absence of thoughts —
the all-pervading peace...
as your true nature... is recognizing the perfection of what you are.

On the absolute level you and love are always one.

On the relative level
you may suffer from separation, from rejection,
from judgment by self or others.

Without running away from the relative
let the absolute be your master
whom you bow to as often as you possibly can.

In the one reality even the absolute and the relative are not separated.

They are simply seen for what they are and appreciated for what they are.

Are you unique?
Most certainly!
Every blade of grass is, every grain of sand.

Are you eternal?
See for yourself.
Why would you not be?

On the direct path you never postpone your homecoming.
You see immediately that home is where you are and when you are.

J. Soós 17 X. 1995

CHAPTER 2.

JÓSKA SOÓS — Universal Shamanism

WHEREVER I HAVE THE opportunity to work in a shamanic way or to *shamanize* — whether in my home office; in my classes in the United States or Europe; during my journeys to India, South America, or Jordan; or at a women's prison — I can effortlessly invoke the presence of Jóska.

My meeting with Jóska Soós (1921–2008) — Hungarian shaman and painter who lived in Belgium after the Second World War — is one of the most influential events in my life. I will never forget it. It took place during a public demonstration he gave in Antwerp in the Fall of 1976.

I had only heard about him a week before. It was a quiet afternoon in my office at the university. As was my custom, my door was open so that students would not hesitate to wander in if they wanted to. One who I barely knew did come in, and to my surprise he asked me to supervise his Master's thesis on Carlos Castaneda.

Nobody knew that I had been devouring his books. In them, Castaneda recounts his adventures as a pupil of Don Yuan Matus, an Indian Yaqui shaman from Mexico. Of course, I was more than happy to delve into a subject that fascinated me. And then, my student told me that a Hungarian shaman living in Brussels planned to give a lecture and session in Antwerp, just a week later. I was dumbfounded. I had no idea there was an active shaman in Belgium.

Jóska had barely started his session when I was already engulfed in an atmosphere that felt both very foreign and at the same time totally familiar. The hairs on both of my arms were standing straight up from deep emotion and recognition.

Especially Jóska's voice made a tremendous impact on me. It seemed to surge up from the bowels of the earth. At that point I had no clue that a human voice could produce such a variety and range of sounds. There were many different animal sounds, especially penetrating frog sounds — more like "cosmic frog." At the same time, he was playing on a number of finely tuned Tibetan bowls. Sounds of the earth were woven into the fabric of the heavenly realms, and vice versa.

At the end of the evening I overcame my shyness to ask Jóska if he was available to work with me. He gave me a look as if he were seeing right into my soul and said, "Yes, every Wednesday evening in Brussels. You really have to come." It was a compelling and commanding invitation. For many years I would take a bus, a train, and a tram to get to his place. It rarely took less than three hours, one way. I did not mind. I had found a master of direct energetic transmission.

First Jóska would take me to his library, which was full of fascinating books on shamanism, mythology and comparative religion. For a minute or so he intuitively tuned in to what was going on with me. Then he would pick one or two books and look for an image he felt was suitable for the occasion — a tantric symbol from Tibetan Buddhism, an Egyptian temple, statues from Easter Island. He would explain the importance or meaning of it and whip himself up in a trance-like enthusiasm. When

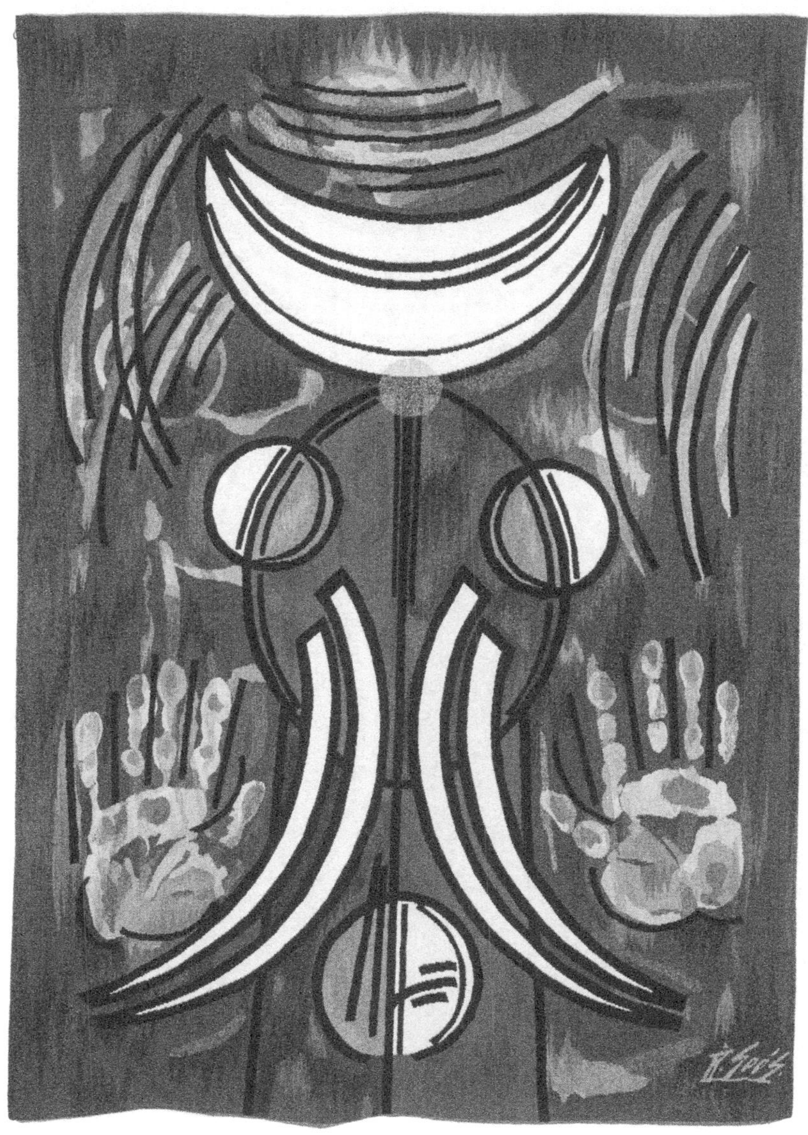

he thought I was "warmed up" sufficiently he would lead me to his workroom.

The actual session, which he always taped, began with Jóska invoking the protective guides and deities of his drum and of himself. He invoked the earth through his drum, the water through some small rattles, the air through little bells, the fire through a big rattle, and the primal sound through a conch. In front of him was a whole series of Tibetan bowls which he played with a variety of mallets. Soon he would hear the appropriate mantra for the situation at hand — for example, a series of seven sounds. He was always able to find the right sounds to bring me back to a state of harmony.

After a session I was fully charged. Everything in my body was flowing, and my emotions were more readily available. Typically, the effect lasted for two to three days, or sometimes longer when I had a private session. I had stumbled into a learning process with an unusually gifted shaman and master of sound.

Jóska was the ideal teacher for me. He was not critical, but always ready to encourage. His formidable knowledge never came from just the intellect — it was connected to his body and his heart. He had deep roots in his Hungarian heritage. At the same time, he was a universal shaman, steeped in Tibetan Buddhism and Taoism. His main driving force was his ambition to give form to the unseen and unheard.

Jóska's house was full of his mysterious and evocative paintings. I was impressed by all of them. After a time, Jóska surprised me by making paintings where he represented us both. (see pages xvi and 16) These were the best gifts I ever received! I am grateful to be able to show many of Jóska's works in this book.

Let me tell you a bit about Jóska's life story, which is full of symbolism and the workings of destiny. He was born in 1921 inside the amniotic sac, an "en-caul" birth. In such a birth, the baby is able to keep breathing without loss of oxygen, and the brain cells responsible for paranormal perception remain intact.

Since he was born in the mystical clan of the Bacsa, and because of the way he was born, the local village shaman, Tamas Bacsi, started his training at the tender age of five. Jóska may very well have been the last Hungarian shaman initiated in the clan of the Bacsa.

He was a very unusual child and would leave his home at night to sit for hours listening and looking at the water flowing through the Danube River. His mother was worried enough to take him to the famous psychoanalyst Sándor Ferenczi, who observed him for a week. He declared him to be a genius and luckily recommended to her and to the school to give the boy plenty of space.

Like so many other Hungarians during the Second World War, Jóska was taken by the Nazis and put in a labor camp when he was in his very early twenties. He saw how many of his compatriots perished there. After the war he became a refugee, since he did not want to go back to his native country. Hungary was to become a satellite state of the Soviet Union, and Jóska's destiny as a shaman and artist was calling him to the West. First he went to look for work in the Netherlands, but after waiting eight months for a work permit, he was denied. He traveled south to Belgium where he started working, in May 1946, in the coal mines of the Ardennes Forest, close to the town of Charleroi. Apparently, the Belgian government had promised that foreign coal miners would receive a passport after two years, since the Belgians themselves were no longer willing to do this dangerous and unhealthy work. However, the promise was not kept. He needed to work for a long five years to get his residential status. This period in the mines would seriously affect his lungs.

Interestingly enough, those difficult life circumstances were perfect for Jóska's development as a shaman and as an artist. As a coal miner, deep in the bowels of Mother Earth and far away from sunlight, he discovered the light in the darkness. Each day he had a 45-minute lunch break, but he chose not to go back up with his colleagues. He turned off his electrical lamp and sat in meditation in the pitch black darkness. One day the figure of Christ appeared in front of him. He was able to draw this. In 1950, he exhibited his work for the first time in the Galerie du Parc in Charleroi. In 1955, his work *Je suis la Résurrection et la vie* received a bronze medal from the city of Paris. Many exhibitions would follow.

When my papers to immigrate to the U.S. came through, I became aware of a deep yearning to receive an initiation from Jóska before I left. The only date available in his busy schedule was the evening before my departure, March 14th, 1985.

It turned into a quite remarkable session. Later I would listen to the recording multiple times. Jóska himself was very enthusiastic about the guides who were offering their assistance. "There are even more present here than during my own initiation!" he claimed.

In those days, Jóska was still living in Brussels and I was lodging with my younger brother Filip in his Antwerp apartment. The initiation session had taken much longer than anticipated, and therefore I called my brother to tell him I would be late. Strangely, I was not able to reach him from Jóska's phone. There was no busy signal either — no contact whatsoever. This had never happened to me. Then Jóska tried, with the same result. We looked at each other, and both of us felt that this was bizarre, and could possibly have a deeper meaning.

I was in a curious state of expanded consciousness as I left Jóska's home. My heart was bursting with love. Everything around me had an eerie intensity. I intuited that my initiation would have far-reaching consequences for my life. When I finally reached the train station on the outskirts of Brussels, I found that I had missed the latest direct train to Antwerp. There was nothing to do except wait for the last slow train...

This was my last evening in Belgium, and who knows when I would be able to return home? While waiting, I saw in the

/Ave-Maria-Stella: H-Viervuldigheid. 1999/

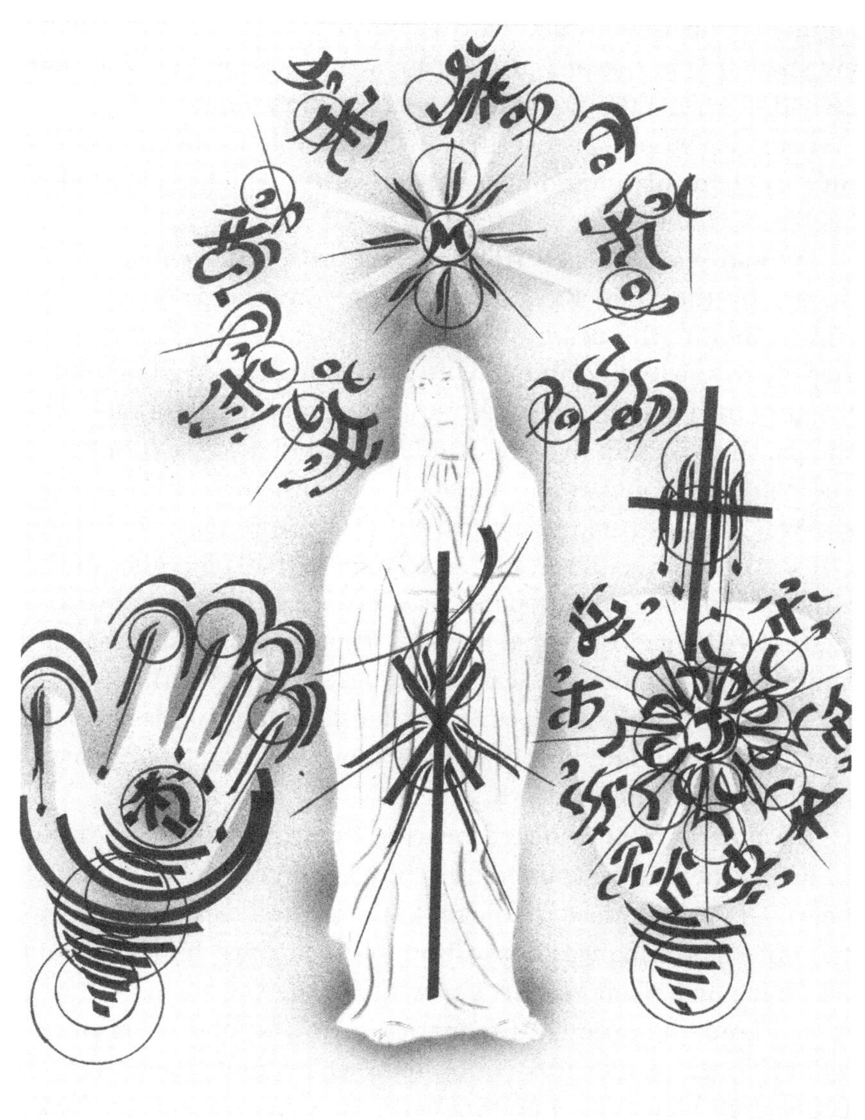

distance a young man purposefully approaching me. He came very close and suddenly addressed me. "Are you a Hare Krishna member?" he asked. I denied this, but felt called to share about my shamanic initiation, and that my teacher explicitly said that he had observed the figure of Krishna around me.

Later we would sit together in the train, and now it was his turn to share his incredible but true story, which had actually been reported in the newspaper.

He had just returned from a castle in southern Belgium — owned by the Hare Krishnas — where they held a service to commemorate the death of his sister. Apparently she had been very open spiritually, and had often tried to pass on some of her insights to her more rationally-inclined brother. Among other things, she told him that she would probably die at a young age, and that he should try to be at peace with this. Even though she was not a formal member of the Hare Krishnas, she would often visit their center. It just so happened that a member of the Krishnas had been ordered to leave because of his disruptive and aggressive behavior; he had been unofficially diagnosed as a paranoid schizophrenic. He was so outraged about this that he had been hiding in the woods around the castle to take his revenge, and chose a random victim. This is how the young man's sister had met her untimely death.

I was extremely shocked hearing this story, and I used our time together on the train to offer him some counseling from the heart. Obviously, this was meant to be my first *task* after my initiation. The timing was not lost on me — in a few hours I would be sitting on a plane to start a new life in the US.

Without the strange disconnection in the phone service, I would not have met this young man. Or would I have? Which (universal?) laws are operating here? How interesting that Jóska and I knew beforehand that something peculiar was going on. I wondered later why this young man thought I would belong to the Hare Krishnas, but that actually was not so mysterious. I carried a little drum that Jóska had painted on. Even more noticeable was the orange garb of an Osho disciple I was wearing at the time.

Looking back, I can say that the empowerment I received during my initiation marked the official beginning of my activities as a shaman. It seems appropriate to say a few words here about the function of *initiation* and its connection to *awakening*.

Awakening itself can take place very suddenly. In the previous chapter, I describe the spontaneous awakening of Ramana Maharshi into a universe of nonduality. All the masters I talk about in this book seem to have gone through episodes of awakening. It can take many years until a breakthrough of awakening stabilizes itself, and a regular, functional life can be resumed.

To prepare for a jump into an awakened life, formal initiations can be offered. They can take a person across an invisible threshold. Amongst native peoples, the ritual of initiation was the preferred method to mark a big transition. The evolution from boy to adult or from girl to woman was painstakingly and respectfully prepared. In virtually all tribes, the initiation of a new shaman was a highlight. Religions have their own initiation rituals. In the Roman Catholic church, for instance, there are the three classic sacraments of initiation: Baptism, Confirmation and Holy Communion.

One can find a good example of a spontaneous initiation/awakening in the biblical story of Paul. He was persecuting the Jewish Christians until one day, on his way to Damascus, he was hit by a blinding light, throwing him off his horse. After that he was never the same. He fell, as it were, into true beingness.

Though it can be very helpful, there is no absolute necessity to receive formal initiations. I personally resonate, though, with the rich tradition of the ancient mystery or initiation schools of Egypt, Greece (Pythagoras, Socrates), India and Tibet

(Padmasambhava). Initiates were secretly prepared to receive access to inner knowledge. Life itself can also do the job and function as a mystery school. The way of the direct path is to be available to what is calling you each moment.

A dear Reiki friend gifted me with a beautiful definition of initiation by the Dutch writer Umtul Valeton-Kiekens: *"Initiation is a grace touching the being of humans through which spiritual development is stimulated in a lifelong embrace."*

On my path, I sometimes come upon misunderstandings about shamanism. Some claim it is just a trendy new age phenomenon. Since I often teach in North America, I encounter some who hold the opinion that only Indians should be entitled to teach it. My own teacher, however, came from a long European tradition.

There is also a growing abundance of archeological evidence that shamanism has been present since the early dawn of humanity. In Burgundy, in the heartland of France, there is a vast prehistoric cave with beautiful shamanic drawings. Kathy and I were collaborating with Lauren Artress, the famous specialist of the Chartres labyrinth, whose book *Walking a Sacred Path* reintroduced the labyrinth as a form of walking meditation. We had decided to take our participants into that cave...

First, we observed the paintings of many different animals. Mammoth is the most common. Then there are bear and rhino, birds and felines. Also, like in so many caves worldwide, *negative* human hands — hand imprints outlined with pigment. They were made 33,000 years ago! Compared to this, ancient Egypt is still young.

In one of the caves, the local cave guide granted me permission to lead a ceremony. I allowed spontaneous sounds and chants to come through while I was beating on my shaman drum. The whole space filled itself with a sacred intensity. Everyone was able to feel presences — of animals, of ancestors, of guides. A clairvoyant in our group was able to give us a blow-by-blow account of what she had been seeing... how the presences came closer, somewhat timidly. How they quickly dispersed when somebody in our group started playing the violin, however beautifully.

Another cave, Chauvet, has recently become very well known. Its drawings are even older — at least 35,000 years old, or painted 20,000 years before Lascaux! This one also is in France, in the Ardèche region in the South. It was discovered in 1994 behind a rock wall that had collapsed many thousands of years ago. The inside was preserved in perfect condition. Not only was humanity given a sudden and unique time capsule, it had the effect of a time bomb on certain beliefs about the past.

Just as with the discovery of the Dead Sea Scrolls and the Nag Hammadi documents in the Middle East after the Second World War, science had to drastically revise some of its theories.

Chauvet changes a great number of assumptions about the mental orientations and capacities of our ancestors from the Stone Age. It comes as a message for our time when we have become so alienated from nature and the undomesticated animals. There are almost 400 drawings in Chauvet. They are not only exquisitely beautiful, but have been executed with such hauntingly moving and masterful craft. Galloping horses, running bisons, fighting rhinos, fantasy beings (such as half woman/half bison). Each moment you almost anticipate they will jump off the wall towards you.

Chauvet seems to arise out of nowhere. Where are its precursors? It starts an unbroken tradition which lasted for at least 20,000 years. It depicts a well-intended world in which humans have great respect for the animal. At that time there were, of course, many more animals than humans. Humans are not yet acting as if they are superior to animals, and have a deep respect for what lives next to them. There is absolutely no sense of a looming ecological disaster.

In this large complex of caves in Chauvet, one of the spaces demonstrates an unmistaken honoring of the cave bear. It is clear that rituals took place here. We even know with certainty that a child of ten entered this space 27,000 years ago! We also know (don't you love science!) that the main artist working in this cave lived 35,000 years ago and had one crooked finger. With the same colors he used to depict the animals, he drenched his own hands to leave imprints on the cave walls.

This phenomenal art can be seen in a great documentary made by German filmmaker Werner Herzog, which he aptly named *Cave of Forgotten Dreams* (2011).

Jóska Soós often distinguished nine spheres of consciousness. For him, these were not just theoretical concepts. He was able to experience these in a visceral manner. They were part of the shamanic practice and cosmology to understand human beings in their totality — to know who they are and what they are able to do. He felt that most of us use few of our capabilities and make little use of the perception of these spheres of consciousness.

1. The personal consciousness starts at conception (prenatal) and contains the events that are turning points in our life.
2. The collective consciousness goes back to the beginning of the human species.
3. The amphibian consciousness goes back even further – some living beings came out of the water and adapted themselves to live on the land.
4. The water consciousness – the life of the fish, larvae, plankton, single-celled organisms.
5. The crystal consciousness – all matter, all atomic and subatomic particles.
6. The light consciousness – photons.
7. The sound consciousness.
8. The aroma – or taste consciousness.
9. The perfume consciousness.

Chauvet

When you die before your physical body dissolves itself
you gain access to eternal life.

Deep meditation, in which you bypass so many identifications,
can serve a similar purpose.

As a shaman you learn to navigate between the dimensions,
between the parallel universes, between past, present and future.

See the synchronicities in history itself.
The beautiful Chauvet cave paintings from 36,000 years ago
can touch the heart of millions of people.

Your effort and your surrender to awaken are not lost in time.
The invisible world of the ancestors, of the power animals,

of the guides and teachers, the Ascended Masters,
is always surrounding you and supporting you.

Mother Earth

What a gigantic presence!
Feel your deep love for the earth
and become one with her.

Become one with all her delightful creatures,
both visible and invisible.

Make sure your roots are extending far into the bosom of Mother Earth
and at the same time let your body be as transparent as possible.

Roots and a transparent body of light make it safe
to navigate between the many dimensions of the one reality.

The original blueprint of the one reality
makes itself known to you
when you are sensitive, open, loving, respectful.
Her invitation is to be with you, right now.

You recognize this as your reality as well.
This is humbling and exhilarating.

Fully expanded, always rooted,
your heart in the center, your spirit soaring,
you are now this gigantic presence.

The art of Jóska Soós: Transmission through the light and sound beings.

I WANT TO ELABORATE a bit more about Jóska's visionary art work, which is displayed throughout this book. Let me first tell you how I started building my personal collection.

In 1990, Kathy and I were able to purchase a modest home in a quiet Portland neighborhood. It was a big step for us. We had to meet with our bankers a few times before they were ready to accept us for a loan. Kathy scored higher than I did; she had a job with a high-tech firm. My profession as a Reiki master and a shaman ("What on earth is a shaman?") was less financially impressive. I am still grateful to the loan officer who gave us the final go-ahead. We had won her over with our enthusiasm, and she intuited, quite rightly, that we might make it as a solid couple...

One of my students, John Nicol, an architect, had met his wife Carillon in a Reiki class I was teaching at Breitenbush Hot Springs. At the end of the class, while taking a group picture, way too many students were sitting on a single massage table

when it collapsed. It was Carillon's table, and John immediately sprinted to the Breitenbush toolshed and fixed her table in no time. That was the beginning of a beautiful romance and long-term marriage! The four of us became good friends. John — who knew our small home quite well, and also the office space I was using outside of my home — had received inner guidance that it was time for us to have a larger, more harmonious space, and that he would both design it and build it for me. In the meantime, the vice-president of our bank had become a regular client of mine. Suddenly, getting a loan for a major remodel (much costlier than the original price for our home) was no problem at all. I still honor John's vision to persuade me and Kathy to see things in a more expanded way. He built space for us based on the principles of sacred geometry. And the space opened itself to receive sacred art...

The next time I went to Belgium and visited Jóska, I bought two paintings of his incredibly haunting and powerful sound and light beings (pages 154 and 208). It was the beginning of a growing collection that would expand as our home later underwent one more major transformation. So many visitors to our home have benefitted from the spiritual transmission emanating from Jóska's work. Whenever I come back from my frequent travels, the light and sound beings are there to greet me and welcome me back into their world of radiance, peace and promise. At this moment, we have 42 works of Jóska's art on display. Our latest acquisition is the largest: a handwoven tapestry (page 61) based on one of his paintings (page 62).

I can honestly say that during my twenties and thirties there was a fair amount of unrest and disconnectedness within me, even though I had become an early and dedicated seeker. As a child I still had an awareness of the dimension of light. It started to dim from excessive studying during my high school and college years. Fortunately, meditation provided many openings for me and led me to remarkable masters. Jóska became the still-point of my search. He was consistently able to empower and stabilize me in between my breakthroughs.

This is how it felt to me — when the ground underneath me was shifting, he would bring me back to earth. When I lost momentum and my search dried up, he would catapult me into the sky.

In his sessions, he frequently used the same power objects. These were his drum, rattles and collection of Tibetan bowls, which he often put on top my head "to make new neuron connections in the brain." All of this literally rattled me and opened me up further, until I had accomplished — with Jóska's help — a fairly complete shamanic soul retrieval. Obviously, this did not happen in one single session. It was more a process that took place during the whole period of my apprenticeship with him.

Worldwide, shamans are known to replace "soul loss" by restoring one's innate power. Soul loss can take place through any number of incidents in our lives that have left some traumatic imprint. I will broadly define "soul retrieval" as a journey from woundedness to wholeness. In my case, it was really a combination of Jóska's voice and his art that sustained me throughout this journey and brought me back home.

I could never get enough of his magical throat singing and the spontaneous mantras arising from faraway corners of the cosmos. Something with a deep thirst and hunger had been lying dormant in me and was now receiving rich nourishment. When he would blow on one of his Tibetan conches, the whole universe would reverberate in the cells of my body.

Jóska would explain how the conch captured the resonance from the Big Bang. And how the conch is also connected with water and "the eternal feminine," as in the mythical birth of Venus, and how all biological life initially came out of the water. When he talked about all this, he would not speak as an academic. He would be the seer reexperiencing the course of evolution, and he would invite me to reexperience that for myself.

His own house was chockfull of his majestic paintings and inspired me to start my own collection. After his sessions, the light and sound beings became even more alive and vibrant. For me they are messengers from a different dimension, a radiant world beyond the earth. His art connected to the very early visual expressions of humanity and also to the contemporary avant-garde. It is art that has a transformational effect on the perceiver. I would say it opens new pathways of perception and creates a bridge to the multidimensional.

In all of Jóska's art, he reveals the emanation of light. He gives titles to thousands of his works, usually in French, and very often there are references to both light and sound. A few examples: *Entité lumineuse sonore, Le chaman transfiguré sonore (prima-terra), Ma mère chérie en son et lumière, Ave-Maria-Stella-Mystique, du Sacré Coeur Cosmosonore.*

My friend, photographer Lloyd Lemmermann, has taken photographs of all Jóska's art in my possession. We intend to put the whole collection on my website so everyone can have access.

Often Jóska paints with an airbrush on canvas. Especially when he uses gold and silver, the look of a painting can vary depending on the amount of sunlight or the angle of viewing. It is as if the paintings are alive and reflect different dimensions. Lloyd has done a wonderful job capturing those effects.

Monique Franken, the wife of Jóska and a shaman in her own right, started organizing exhibitions of his works after his death. Often she collaborates with Tamara Ingels, who dedicated a major part of her Ph.D. on Jóska's art. Whenever possible, Kathy and I and our shamanic students would join Monique at the exhibitions in the hospice house where Jóska spent his last months. We would chant and drum together, and it has become a healing highlight for the people staying there. The nurse who took care of Jóska is instrumental in using these occasions as a form of art therapy. In a way, she was his last student. The beneficial effects from these events — and from his works that hang there — are obvious.

On page 232 you can see a self-portrait of Jóska which he called *La Vision d'Ezechiel – autoportrait*. It looks exactly like an older version of him in the guise of the biblical prophet Ezekiel. He seems to be pointing to a new, golden age...

CHAPTER 3.

MIKAO USUI — Reiki

In April of 2016, I stood in front of an audience of 150 people in Brussels at the *30 years Reiki in Belgium* celebration. Many Belgians were present, of course, and also Reiki practitioners from Holland, Germany, France, Russia and Iran. I had received a special invitation, because long ago I was one of the first Reiki instructors to come and teach regularly in Belgium, and I have never stopped.

I gave a hug to many of my students, some of whom I had not seen for years. My heart was filled with joy. The celebration was especially poignant because people were still reeling from the Isis bombings at the Brussels airport just a couple of weeks before. There was an urgent need for people to be together in a heart-to-heart way.

My Reiki story started thirty years earlier at the Oregon School of Massage, where I had registered as a student after my time with Osho. At the end of a massage exchange, my friend Joel Saxe asked me if he could also give me a bit of Reiki. I had never heard of Reiki, but was interested. In less than five minutes I felt something vast coming through his hands, and I was very intrigued — what was that? I could not wait to hunt down this fresh trail and find out more.

Soon after this experience, I took a class with Paul Mitchell, who had himself studied Reiki with Hawayo Takata, the first person to introduce Reiki from Japan to the West in 1937.

In its origin, Reiki is an art of healing which uses a series of laying-on-of-hands positions. At the same time, it is a way to connect with cosmic, universal life energy. The founder is Dr. Mikao Usui (1865–1926), a Buddhist monk who also had a deep heart connection with Jesus.

In 1994, a memorial stone dedicated to Mikao Usui was discovered at the Saihoji Temple site in Japan. It had been erected by his students a year after his death and has details about his life and vision chiseled on it. It mentions that Usui called his method a secret path to happiness:

The Reiki method is not only for curing illness. Its true purpose is to correct the heartmind, keep the body fit, and lead a happy life using the spiritual capabilities human beings were endowed with since birth.

Usui's vision connects to the time in which we are now living. Less than a hundred years after his death, there are millions of active Reiki practitioners, working in almost all the countries in the world. This specific form of laying-on-of-hands healing is being used in many hospitals as a complimentary form of therapy. And, it is being offered in crisis situations, such as refugee camps.

The so-called Reiki principles, as formulated by Usui and translated by Mrs. Takata, are very simple:

- Just for today, do not worry.
- Just for today, do not anger.
- Honor your parents, teachers and elders.
- Earn your living honestly.
- Show gratitude to every living thing.

When you meet Reiki practitioners they often tell one interesting story after another. I will share a couple from my own life.

One day I received an anxious phone call from my mother in Belgium. She was worried about the mental and emotional state of my father and asked me to try to help him during my upcoming visit. This had never happened before — my dad had never tended towards depression. True, he was getting older; he was just past eighty.

When I came home from the U.S. I went to my parents' house straightaway. As always, they were very happy to see me. I could see that my dad was lacking vigor, and when I proposed a Reiki session he responded enthusiastically. This was remarkable! Many years prior I had given him Reiki, and to my disappointment I had the impression that he did not enjoy it.

My father was lying on the couch in the living room. After 15 minutes of following the formal sequence of positions I experienced a strong pull to take his left hand into both of my hands. Uncharacteristically, he began to sob. He apologized, and I assured him that it was quite all right to cry. In the meantime, I could not control my own tears. Neither could my mother, who was watching all this from a distance.

Afterwards, my father shared with me the memory that surfaced, a secret which he felt terribly guilty about. His father — and all our family knew this — had worked for the railway, and there had been a horrible bombing of his station by the allies at the end of World War II. He saw many people dying around him. My grandfather, who was a very sensitive man, never recovered from this trauma. After this event he rarely spoke to anybody and gradually retreated from the world.

Now, for the first time, my father told me what took place the night his father died. He was suffering intensely, and my grandmother had arranged for the doctor to come. Only she and my father were at home. The doctor evaluated what was going on and asked my father if it would be okay to "help his father a bit."

My grandmother and my father said yes, and after an injection my grandfather quickly passed away. Apparently, my father's conscience had never come to terms with this and he had a strong need to share it.

I remember that my grandfather would hardly ever touch people. Neither did my dad. I know that I suffered from this as a teenager when my father's touching disappeared altogether. One of my Reiki students once jokingly remarked that my becoming a professional massage therapist and Reiki practitioner was a classic example of Freud's compensation theory. There is certainly some truth in this! I also think that in our wound, a gift is hiding, waiting to be transformed. To illustrate this, I will return now to the Reiki session I gave to my dad.

The only time my grandfather had grabbed and touched the hands of my father was on that hellish night of his passing. Many, many years later, during the Reiki session, I took my father's hand in a loving and caring way. I had never done this before. In a flash a healing took place, on a cellular level, of my masculine lineage. Not surprisingly, my father's depression lifted almost immediately. I was walking on a cloud for days. For a very long time I had yearned to have more intimate contact with my dad. Also, it turned out my mother was absolutely right. She just *knew* that I was the one who could help my father.

The Reiki path is not without its challenges. Shortly after taking the Second Degree Reiki class, I was suffering from severe back trouble. The pain was so intense I had to crawl on hands and knees to reach the bathroom. I strongly suspected that unconscious factors were at play, but I had no idea what they could possibly be. I started to have doubts about my "life path." I had felt so guided and supported, and now this...! At the time I was earning my living as a massage therapist, so this back pain did not bode well.

Martie, the wife of my Reiki Master, suggested giving me Reiki sessions four days in a row. This is often done in difficult situations. Each day the treatment goes in at a deeper level, and finally there is more clarity, insight and healing of the cause. Sure enough, there was more there than I had suspected.

A loneliness had crept into me after I had finally moved for good to the U.S., regarding friendships with men. In Belgium, most of my colleagues and friends were male. It was not easy for me to "get" the average American male. In a final attempt to find some friends, I had joined a sports club where I could play racket ball. I had similar issues there, until I met a kind man from South America who seemed happy to play a game with me. But on the day of our agreed-upon appointment he failed to show up. Instead, I was assigned a woman — a woman in the midst of a nasty divorce — as a partner. Apparently, the combination of her angry vibes and the depth of my disappointment over yet another failed friendship had created fertile ground to generate my back pain. In a flash, during the Reiki treatment, I re-experienced the physical and psychological pain that I had been repressing.

And there was much more. The deepest pain and blockages were buried in yet another layer of repression. It all came to me in the fourth session. In the very moment of my first Reiki class, maybe even during the five minutes I had received Reiki at the massage school, there was a soul recognition. Something told me that I had been waiting for this my whole life. Somehow, I already knew that I was meant to continue all the way to becoming a Reiki master (the Third Degree of Reiki) But in my unconscious mind, two gigantic hurdles were blocking this path.

The first blockage had to do with money. It can be quite expensive to become a master in the lineage of my choice, and I was not yet able to give myself permission to invest in my future in this way. Now I can clearly see this as a form of strictness, or lack of love towards my own deep longing.

The second blockage is easier to guess — fear. This fear took a number of forms. The fear that I was not good enough to transmit

Reiki at the highest level. Fear around the responsibility of being a teacher. Fear that my life would spiral into a bustling current I would not be able to control.

Now, looking back at that critical period in my life, I see of course the lesson. My life path had brought me so close to the door of happiness. Yet I was unable to cross the threshold because of my own fears and resistance. When the pain and desperation became unbearable, I was willing to seek and accept help. The (cosmic) joke is of course that all this became the best preparation for being a teacher. What I have experienced myself, I can help others to see if they are still struggling.

The silence of Reiki

The silence of Reiki is full of life and new creation.

Reiki touches the richness and abundance residing inside of you.

Reiki honors and respects what you are.

When you no longer limit Reiki,
you will not experience yourself as limited.

The voice of Reiki is asking you —
What does life want from you?

Being willing to answer this question
launches you on a journey that never ends.

When you take this journey
you understand deeply why you are here.

Reiki is surrendering to Love.

The great master healers

Become a good friend with your own heart
It will take care of you and it will teach you everything.

As a new consciousness is getting a stronger foothold on the planet
it carries the beauty of the aspirations of all of you.

Many masters have pioneered the path before you
and now you are being called into mastery.

Mastery is the ability to be in alignment with your true destiny.

Embracing your true destiny brings you authentic happiness.

When you are happy you are an open vessel for creative consciousness.

The divine feminine is a fundamental aspect of creative consciousness.

It inspires so many forms of alternative healing.
They are all based on love and a deep respect for intuition
and for the wisdom inherent in nature itself.

Be free and choose a healing path that fits with what you are.

All healing ways arise from oneness and present you with your own unique path to consciously return to oneness.

You are the healers of the world because you care and because of what you are.

As you bless the world, you are being blessed.

Growing into mastery is finding great delight in service.

The great master healers — the Buddha, Jesus, Krishna, Padmasambhava, Dr. Mikao Usui — have never disappeared.

Their presence is getting stronger as you become more sensitive.

The female healers are joining you now.
Lakshmi, Kwan Yin, Saraswati, Sweet Mother,
Mother Meera, Mother Mary, Mrs. Takata.

Honor what you are and honor the preciousness of all beings.

Please know that the light of what you are can never be extinguished.

All your hearts are working in unison now so that the new frequency can be received by many in a clear and pure fashion.

In deep gratitude for sharing these sacred times of transformation.

Creation is ongoing.
Your intentions and your aspirations are ushering in the new consciousness.

CHAPTER 4.

GURDJIEFF — Self-Remembering

RIGHT NOW, WHILE YOU are reading this, can you pause and become aware — for a moment — of what is surrounding you right now in your precious life? Later I will speak more about this practice, one of the many things I learned from Gurdjieff. He famously said, *"Remember yourself always and everywhere."*

Many consider Georgi Ivanovitch Gurdjieff (1866–1949) as the foremost pioneer of the New Age in the West, and he is known as the discoverer of the enneagram. I strongly recommend that you watch the movie *Meetings with Remarkable Men* (1979), directed by the famous British theatre director Peter Brook, based on Gurdjieff's autobiography.

I was very moved by the opening scene, which takes place in a valley surrounded by high mountains. The young Gurdjieff is with his father in Afghanistan and they witness a competition between people who are singing or playing native instruments.

At a certain moment, an answer comes from the mountains. An enormous overtone rolls around the whole valley and echoes for a long time. The young Gurdjieff is overcome by a quiet and strong emotion. It is one of innumerable meetings with remarkable men on his life path.

Gurdjieff was born in the Caucasus on the border of Turkey and Russia, the son of an Armenian mother and a Greek father. From early childhood he felt a strong need to come to grips with the meaning of human existence. His father, a wise man in his own right, became his first teacher. He soon saw that neither science nor religion was very helpful in explaining the big issues of life and death. Because they started from different premises, they also came to different conclusions. Gurdjieff had an inner certainty that a real knowledge about these existential questions must have existed in ancient times, and that this knowledge was most likely handed down through oral tradition from one generation to the next. In his younger years he took part in expeditions in search of this knowledge...

During Gurdjieff's stay in spiritual communities in Central Asia, he witnessed the holy temple dances and dervish dances. Why are they *holy*? The movements of the dancers are very precise. The combinations of the movements and their rhythm represent a language expressing the fundamental laws of the cosmos.

Gurdjieff taught his students these *movements* to make them conscious of the different functions — feeling, thinking and moving. When one is able to integrate the three functions in the right way, one experiences a miraculous feeling of totality and unity. All the movements engage the main body parts — legs, arms, head; all are doing something. When these parts are used at the same time, sometimes the head is moving in one particular rhythm while the legs and/or arms are executing a different one. You can imagine how this develops a better attention and a balance between the three centers (feeling, thinking, moving). There are many reports of students about how they would experience the extraordinary feeling that comes by actually being in a different world, when, even for half a minute, one does a movement *correctly*.

Near the end of the movie *Meetings with Remarkable Men,* there is another scene that I love to watch again and again. It is a reconstruction of the *movements* by Jeanne de Salzmann. She met Gurdjieff in 1919 and became totally committed to his work, staying with him until his death in Paris in 1949. For the next forty years she would establish centers in Paris, New York, London and Venezuela where the *movements* were practiced. She died in Paris in 1990 at the age of 101, as Gurdjieff predicted she would.

As with so many others who would meet Gurdjieff, the first impression of him was unforgettable:

> *The presence of Gurdjieff, and especially his penetrating look, made an extraordinary impression. You felt that you were truly seen, exposed by a vision that left nothing in shadow, and at the same time you were not judged or condemned. A relationship was immediately established which removed all fear and at the same time brought you face to face with your own reality. (Jeanne de Salzmann, The Reality of Being: The Fourth Way of Gurdjieff)*

Gurdjieff became the moving spirit of a group calling themselves *The Brotherhood of the Seekers of Truth.* With some of them he went to Egypt, Morocco, India and Afghanistan. Wherever he went he found something of value. He recognized the deepest knowledge in some Sufi communities. The pieces of the puzzle came together for him when he discovered the *enneagram,* a symbol that brings together three universal laws. Gurdjieff never gave explicit information about his sources, but some of his students maintained that he learned it from Sufis in Asia. There are no references to it in Sufi literature (... which is often explained by the fact that it was a secret knowledge passed on by word of mouth).

Gurdjieff presents the enneagram as an all-encompassing representation of the harmonious structure and inner dynamism of the cosmos. It is a triangle within a circle with nine equal parts.

He saw it as a schematic diagram of perpetual motion, a machine of eternal movement. It represents the great forces that drive the human search on planet earth.

The law of one – everything is one and connected together.

The law of three – from the oneness arises the manifestation of a tri-unity. Everything that arises comes from the interaction of three forces — active, passive and reconciling.

The law of seven – the figure of the hexagram which shows how everything is subject to change in dynamic movements.

Everything is one, and in the universe, these three laws are always working together.

The brilliance of Gurdjieff was the ability to use this schema to point to a possible evolution of humanity in terms of "being."

Gurdjieff will certainly be remembered as the one who introduced the enneagram to the West in 1920. Many have elaborated on it since then and use it also as a psychological typology of nine personality types (Helen Palmer, *The Enneagram*):

One is The Perfectionist
Two is The Giver
Three is The Performer
Four is The Tragic Romantic
Five is The Observer
Six is The Trooper
Seven is The Epicure
Eight is The Boss
Nine is The Mediator

When I was 22, the book *In Search of the Miraculous*, by Gurdjieff's Russian disciple Peter D. Ouspensky (1878–1947), suddenly opened a door for me. The subtitle of his book is intriguing: *Fragments of an Unknown Teaching*. For many readers, even today, this remains the book of choice when they approach Gurdjieff's teaching for the first time. It certainly worked for me. It is a brilliantly written account of the essence of self-remembering.

To this day, I am fascinated by the figure and enigma that Gurdjieff was. It becomes clear when reading about him how he changed as a human being after his wanderings. Not only did he find what he was looking for, but he became this knowing, he embodied it. He spent the rest of his life on his mission: to transmit this knowledge in a form that was appropriate for that time and for western culture. He wanted to take his fellow human beings to inner freedom and awakening.

His concept of self-remembrance, as an antidote to being constantly in a sort of sleepy trance state, entered me suddenly and strongly. Just by reading this book, I realized the difference between executing the common routine of daily life or the option to be — at the same time — consciously present in it.

I became very serious about this realization and vowed to myself to try to remember what I am as often as I possibly could.

The first day of my vow I actually succeeded in doing this a couple of times. Then I would completely forget about it all for at least a week. When I noticed that I had forgotten, I immediately renewed my vow of self-remembrance but would forget about it almost as quickly. For many months, and probably many years, this struggle would go on.

And yet I noticed a bit of evolution. Often when I was riding my bicycle, it happened out of the blue. Now I see that the physical activity of bike riding shifted my attention from my head to my body. I would become more and more aware than I could not *forcibly* self-remember. Most often it happened spontaneously — a gift of grace, out of nowhere.

Hello! Once again, could you become aware of what is surrounding you right now? Are you able to harness your will to become as conscious as possible of where you are and what you are? Just give this an honest try.

This could become a good technique to interrupt the daily trance and to notice the bright blue sky behind the fog of the continuous mind stream.

I guarantee that when you succeed in this a number of times, it will help you tremendously to be much more present for yourself and for your precious life.

Gurdjieff respected traditional religions and practices, especially when they were concerned with spiritual transformation. He maintained that every spiritual path has as a goal to create an immortal soul. Each "way" tries to reach this by its own method. He saw that there were three usual categories of approach, and called his own the Fourth Way.

The First way is that of the fakir, a Muslim or Hindu ascetic, who attempts to conquer his body, especially his desires. In the Second way the monk struggles and works on his emotional center. It is the way of devotion, of the heart, of faith. The Third way is that of the yogi who develops and tries to control his intellectual center, his mind. Gurdjieff's observation of the yogi was "he knows everything but can do nothing." In order to do, he must also develop his physical and emotional centers.

What these three ways have in common is the practice of renunciation. Traditionally one must give up family and home and all attachments. In the Fourth way, however, there is no renunciation. On the contrary, one profits from working in the midst of life. It is a way in life and through life. It is also the way of the "skillful" person. That person certainly has some experience with the other ways and benefits from them. But he is not fanatic or dogmatic about it. He picks and chooses as consciously as possible what fits best in his own evolution.

What is always present in the Fourth way is the self-remembering. It is being able to sense the self physically, really inhabiting the body in a way that we are not used to. Beyond that there is an effort to be so present that we are not constantly taken into a dreamy world of free association. Our attention is rarely in the Now. The most important tool for self-remembering is returning again and again to the present moment.

I will finish this chapter by letting some of his close pupils say something about their teacher. I start with Jeanne de Salzmann, whose first impression of meeting Gurdjieff you have already seen.

Jeanne de Salzmann:
(from *The Reality of Being*)

When I met George Ivanovitch Gurdjieff I was thirty years old and living in the Caucasus mountain region of what was then southern Russia. At the time I had a deep need to understand the meaning of life but was dissatisfied with explanations that seemed theoretical, not really useful. The first impression of Gurdjieff was very strong, unforgettable. He had an expression I had never seen, and an intelligence, a force, that was different, not the usual intelligence of the thinking mind but a vision that could see everything. He was, at the same time, kind and very, very demanding. You felt he would see you and show you what you were in a way you would never forget in your whole life... He was like an irresistible force, not dependent on any one form but continually giving birth to forms.

John Bennett:
(from *The Way to be Free*)

If I look back, I have to say that without Gurdjieff I would be very small indeed and it was largely through having the benefit of his most extraordinary search and sacrifice that I and others have had possibilities.

Not everything came from him, but the possibility of making use of what I found, I owe very much to him. This isn't to say that he didn't make mistakes, or that he found the best way of helping people in this day and age. But he was a pioneer of extraordinary courage — daring one might say — he tried things that people had not tried before and under different conditions of life than we have here.

Thanks to his having been willing to expose himself to extreme dangers and a kind of suffering that is not easy to understand, things were opened up for us. But it is totally foolish to think of him as infallible. Even the perfected man is not free from mistakes. The further one goes, the more pitfalls...

And finally, here is Elizabeth Bennett's first impression in 1924, just a few days after Gurdjieff's near-fatal car accident when he had been lying near death in a coma. (from *My Life, J.G. Bennett and G.I. Gurdjieff*)

As he came, he looked directly at me, and all my former ideas and expectations fell away and never returned. How could anyone be afraid of this being? His grave, rather sad face was dark complexioned, and darker now with extensive bruises, but his eyes, large, dark and sparkling beneath his massive brow and the great dome of his shaven head, expressed nothing but compassion. I have never seen a creature more beautiful, more radiant of love and understanding. He could not, I thought, be of this world. From that moment I loved him.

When he recovered from his injuries, he was once more the enigmatic, ironic, contradictory Gurdjieff of whom I had heard so many anecdotes, but in those first days of my meeting him he had need of all his powers to keep his body in action: he could not also play a role or wear a mask. But his later extravagant and occasionally outrageous behavior could never eradicate my first impression.

Some seeds which Gurdjieff planted in my soul:

- If I want to be present I need to really dare to see to what extent I find myself in a state of sleep.
- Attention is a conscious force, a force of consciousness itself. It is a divine force.
- The body has absorbed a number of habits which facilitate my state of sleep. With the proper bodily posture, the different centers can come into harmony. For this it is necessary to have a constant collaboration between my thoughts, my feelings and my body.
- When I try to force something, it comes from the ego. I cannot allow myself to be fooled by an ideal of perfection imposed by thinking.
- To further develop myself, my essence has to come more forward, even when there is an intense resistance from the personality.

Pay attention

It can be really enlivening to pay attention,
not so much to the stream of thoughts
but to the gaps between the thoughts.
They can be sudden and subtle.
You will find them.
They are really there.

In this way fear of emptiness starts to disappear.

What is formless is not empty.
It is alive with overwhelmingly loving presence.

All questions vanish in the silence of this presence.

In the midst of strife and attack
this presence sustains you
as it sustains all life.

This presence is your real self.

When you do not lose sight of this
everything you do is a meditation.

As you are able to embrace your real self
a radius of peace extends all around you
in which many things come into harmony.

As your current form becomes more transparent
your essence is very apparent.

Only love is.

Your essence

In the silence of your loving heart
you automatically discover unlimited,
intelligent and peaceful space, lots of space.

It is very comforting to know that that space is always there.

When you are in that open space, sooner or later,
a number of fundamental questions will arise,
from very deep inside of you.

Are you aware of the difference between your personality and your essence?

If you are — are you willing to lead a life based on your essence?

Can you see that such a willingness would present you
with choices, alternatives, invitations?

Can you see that your choices and stance
would influence the quality of life on this planet?

Are you willing to be guided by love, by truth, by beauty and by justice?

Your willingness is the choice.
Now manifestation can take place.

Your inner transformation is the result of a series of choices
inspired by listening to your essence.

Sitting quietly, meditatively, centered, attentively, relaxed,
gives your essence a chance to be in the foreground.

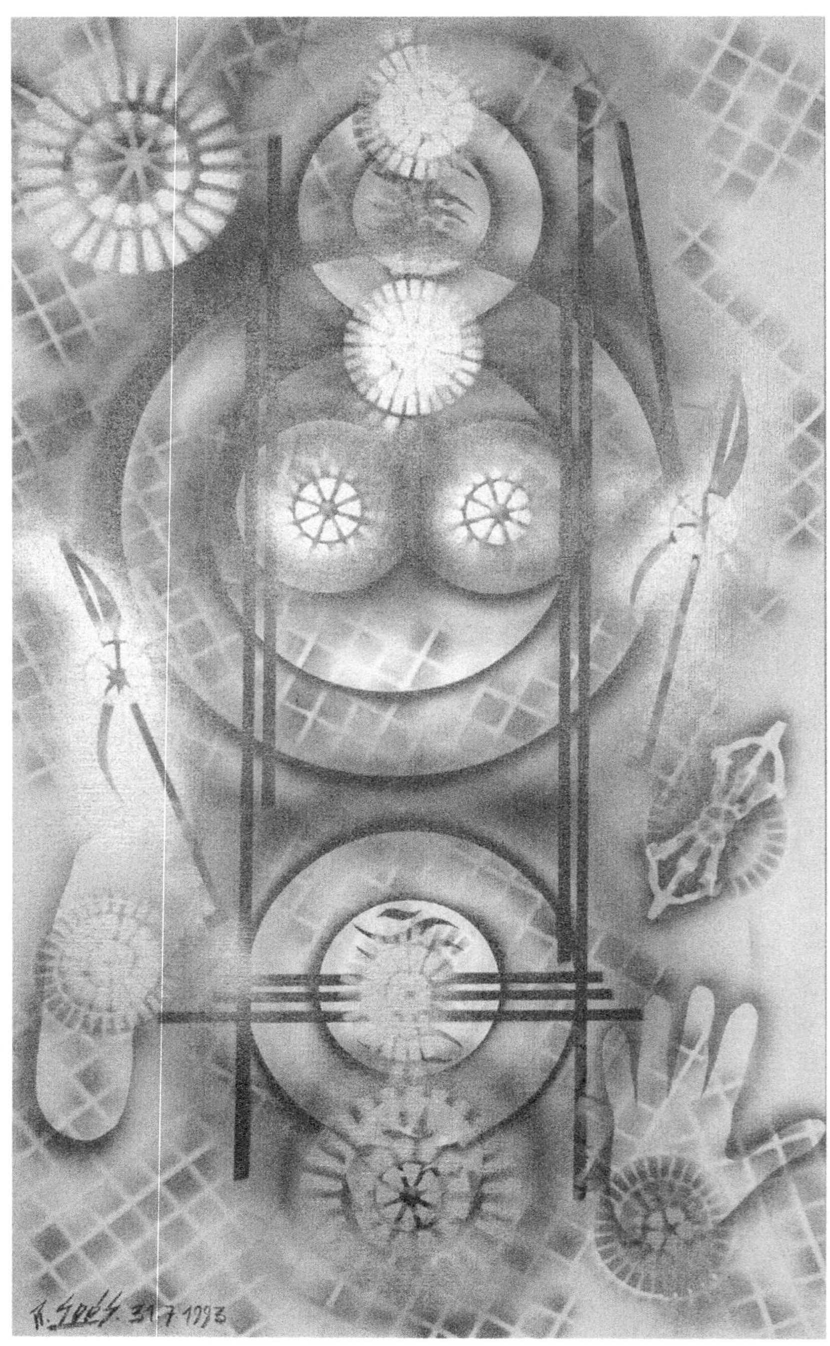

CHAPTER 5.

JERZY GROTOWSKI — Improvisation and the Source of Creativity

AFTER MIDNIGHT, IN A pitch-dark forest somewhere in Poland, I am running very close behind a shaman. I have to follow close on his heels or else the person running behind me will collide with my back. We are a small group of seven runners. One shaman is taking the lead, another one is closing the ranks. In between them are me and four others.

Why am I involved in this? It is not an easy task. It is an exercise in the development of trust and attention. The intention is to learn how to open my senses and to go beyond my fears. Am I afraid? You bet I am. I am not much of a hero to begin with, and certainly not on the physical plane.

In the days leading up to this, I did see that the shamans knew the forest inside out. They had been preparing for this project for three months. Sometimes I saw them running blindfolded through it, very agile and fast. This gave me trust. They really knew what they were doing. But still...

At a certain moment it happens. I surrender; I let go. Fear is gone. I fly like a bird behind the shaman. I am tasting an unknown freedom, also a glimpse of a dimension where anything is possible. Do I have to pay a price for this? Not really. Would I have been able to do this without the support and the dedication of the shamans? Certainly not. Did the fear come back later? Naturally! But the mechanism has been exposed to me, once and for all. Not just as a concept. As an experience. Whenever I meet a feeling of anxiety, whenever I have to become vulnerable, I have to pass through the same gate. The gate is no longer shut tight, and that makes a big difference!

It was a great honor for me to work with Grotowski himself in the woods of Poland. There I could see him more in his role of shaman and also of mystic and sage. Around Richard Schechner at NYU, I witnessed him as theatre historian, philosopher and innovator.

And of course, working as an associate professor in the performance arts at the University of Antwerp, Belgium, I was very familiar with the tremendous scope of work of Jerzy Grotowski (1933–1999). There was no way around him. At that time in the early '70s, he was the most famous innovator in the avant-garde theatre, a true genius. Everybody knew "Grot." He launched the concepts of *theatre laboratory* and *poor theatre*. Grotowski felt that the acceptance of poverty in the theatre would strip it of all that is not essential to it. It would reveal the deep riches which lie in the very nature of this art form.

As the British theatre director Peter Brook wrote,

> *Grotowski makes poverty an ideal; his actors have given up everything except their own bodies; they have the human instrument and limitless time — no wonder they feel the richest theatre in the world.*

Ludwik Flaszen, his artistic director, would describe the goal of their search as follows:

> *Grotowski's productions aim to bring back a utopia of those elementary experiences provoked by collective ritual, in which the community dreamed ecstatically of its own essence, of its place in a total, undifferentiated reality, where Beauty did not differ from Truth, emotion from intellect, spirit from body, joy from pain; where the individual seemed to feel a connection with the Whole of Being.*

Grotowski's unique approach to training actors was intensely physical and improvisational. He wanted to take his research into a deeper realm. At the height of his worldly fame, he did not hesitate to follow his true passion — so stopped making big public productions and opened his work for people who were ready to delve into the sources of creativity. This made a very deep impression on me. The project in the Polish woods belongs to a later phase in his work, which was talked about extensively in the movie *My Dinner with André* (1981, directed by Louis Malle). I was one of the few chosen to participate...

On the Antwerp campus where I was teaching, I had started the *Center for Experimental Theatre.* We were able to invite all the close collaborators of Grotowski to come and teach workshops, one after the other. Certainly, in Belgium those days, this was a true "coup de théâtre." It was a unique opportunity for my students to have firsthand experience with something beyond theatre — something about the art of living in the present and in the body.

Improvisation as a theatre exercise develops the capacity to be spontaneously in the here and now. By spending many hundreds of hours practicing these, I learned to trust that each impulse coming from the body, however minimal, has its own spark of creativity and intelligence. It is often said that the body cannot lie. I personally have experienced the body as a messenger many times... this has greatly helped on my life path.

For example, one day I received something in the mail about a healing and personal transformation center called the East West Centre, close to the abbey of Orval, Belgium. I quickly scanned the information and was going to throw it in my recycling basket. There was a slight nudge holding back my arm. The impulse definitely came from within my body, not from the outside. I gave the information a second look and followed the trail... and now have been teaching there for 20 years.

When I invited Grotowski's colleagues, I also participated in all the workshops. My favorite teacher was Ludwik Flaszen (b. 1930). He became my first true teacher, by recognizing the potential beyond the limitations of my fears and conditionings. Flaszen was a driving force of Grotowski's Laboratory Theatre and its artistic director. His specialty was voice work, and he understood the art of taking people to their authentic voice. Speaking of fear! During my first workshop with him I was constantly confronted by my (perceived) limitations.

We had to work very hard physically. Often, we would toil from midnight till six in the morning. The first hour was an intense warm-up to loosen up and "articulate" all the joints in our bodies. There was a lot of crawling on the floor, followed by jumping up and down. There was sweating and even more sweating. Besides purification, the purpose was to make the body more open. Also, to push beyond our boundaries. Beyond the boundary of fatigue, a reservoir of fresh energy is waiting to be tapped. In the beginning, I just could not do it. I was seriously blocked. I could hear voice breakthroughs in most of the other participants, but I could not get there myself. When a person's authentic voice surfaced, it was as if one or multiple angels started to sing through somebody's voice box. It gave me the chills. It was very humbling to see and hear my students perform much better than I did.

Still, I would not give up. Ludwik himself was very patient with me. I am so grateful he did not give up on me; he was able to see beyond my limitations. From him I learned the beautiful role of the teacher as a midwife. A true teacher can see what the student cannot yet see, and keeps encouraging until there is a new birth.

I would work with Ludwik three more times. The second time a breakthrough took place. The third time I met — once again — this high brick wall. Of course, this was very frustrating. The fourth time I was able to climb or jump several times over that wall. From then on it became much easier to use my authentic voice, and also in a shamanic way.

A really beautiful memory is my participation in a workshop with Jacques Chwat, who often was the official interpreter for Grotowski. We had permission from the academic authorities to use an abandoned and empty fortress on the campus for our theatre experiments. The fortress was one of many that had been built around Antwerp in the time of Napoleon. For a whole week we retreated here, mostly in silence. We did our voice work in the courtyard or in one of the many empty rooms. We were far away from where people were living, and that created a special atmosphere and gave us total freedom to explore, or so we thought. One night we were shocked when the police suddenly showed up. On their rounds, they heard strange vocal sounds coming from the fortress and came to check it out. They took me to my university office, where I had to show them a document that we were entitled to be there. It was a strange juxtaposition of two worlds. When I returned to our group I was even more appreciative of the holy silence there. Jacques Chwat told me later that he had never before led such a beautiful group. That made me very happy.

What was Grotowski's influence on me? He was not only an incredibly gifted theatre maker, but also a culture critic and philosopher. He was able to connect very precise theatre techniques with general observations about life and creativity. Twenty years after his death, these make more sense than ever.

I would like to elaborate on Grotowski's thinking in relation to our current situation, which can feel quite oppressive in so many ways. Is there any silence left anywhere?

We live in a culture of material goods that can easily be reproduced. We have the ability to capture images, sounds, or conversations almost anywhere and anytime, as well as almost continually being within reach of a wide range of messages. This aspect of modern culture can seriously affect our experiences. Invariably, a host of side thoughts arise, which tend to take on a life of their own. In the middle of a remarkable experience, we might think, *How will I be able to describe or explain this to a person who is not here?*

It is exactly future-oriented preoccupations like these that can hinder us from staying present in the moment. To take non-stop pictures or selfies can be a conscious or an unconscious choice. It can take us out of direct experiencing, or not.

Whenever I teach a workshop these days and there is a wi-fi connection, everyone — myself included — will check a wide range of messages. This dramatic change in the last decade has become the norm. What is next?

To what do we really want to be present? I often ask myself such questions. You too, dear reader?

Here is another reflection of Grotowski's ideas, slightly adapted:

Modern civilization has robbed humans of their ecological home, and of a consciousness — or awareness — that they are present as part of the big universe of creation. We have been uprooted and cut off from what were once the natural connections with the environment.

In 1984, during my very last attempt to reconcile my university career with my search for my true vocation, I took the train from Belgium to Italy. I participated for a brief time in a more reclusive phase of Grotowski's work in a small village close to Pontedera. It offered seclusion, but not an escape or refuge from the world. All the work and most of the daily interactions took place in silence and deep concentration. I chose to start out each time with a couple of hours of whirling, like the Sufi dervishes practice. Once again, Grotowski had created a laboratory where experiences could mature without the pressure to ever give a public performance. After a few days, I came to a profound still-point and knew that my next step could only be a jump into the unknown.

I would like to share a quote here from Grotowski, since he talks about warriorship.

> *When I use the term: warrior, maybe you will refer it to Castaneda, but all scriptures speak of the warrior. You can find him in the Hindu tradition as well as in the African one. He is somebody who is conscious of his own mortality. If it's necessary to confront corpses, he confronts them, but if it's not necessary to kill, he doesn't kill. Among the Indians of the New World it was said that between two battles, the warrior has a tender heart, like a young girl. To conquer knowledge he fights, because the pulsation of life becomes stronger and more articulated in moments of great intensity, of danger.*

Your history

Your history has no real importance.
At this moment existence is happy to shower you
with love, abundance and total acceptance.

Imagine you are a tall tree.
You are able to feel the pulse of Mother Earth.
Father Sky is gently caressing your crown.
You are not rushing towards the future.
You have no regrets about the past.
You do not worry how long your life will last.
You are in tune with **all** *that is*
and every moment is a meditation.

The realm of being has no tension.
It ripples out until you are a vast expansion.

Everything is welcome here
and nothing has to happen.
You are the observer and the observed
in a peaceful suspension.

Take care to guard the silence.
It is so restful and festive and very transformative.

Without your history,
without your future,
there is the brightness of this golden moment.
This **is** *eternity.*

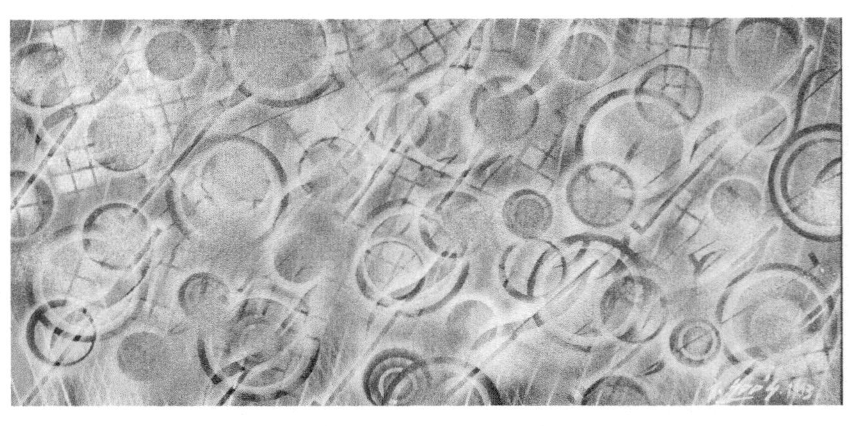

CHAPTER 6.

OSHO — Joy

HE IS STILL SMILING at me, that crazy, always chuckling, wise Osho (1931–1990). I spent two years in his presence. However, this was not a laughing matter. Often it was like going through hell in order to get to heaven.

I enjoy, dear Osho, addressing you personally and directly now. Even when it was still possible, I did not dare to write many letters to you. Shyness prevented me. I did talk to you a fair amount in my head, and sometimes your distinctive voice would answer me. Occasionally you still do.

I learned so much from you — you were such a decisive influence on my life path. You named me Swami Deva Krishna. Though I have been going by Frank again for a long time now, the name change was very beneficial.

You led me from self-consciousness to Consciousness itself. Your unique movement meditations gave me a good shaking. During your *Dynamic Meditation,* almost daily for a long year, I shouted through my pain until it was gone. Nobody had an inkling that so much pain was even there, least of all me.

You could not care less about the prevailing norms and forms. This was often held against you. You made fun of spiritual teachers and trashed politicians, but sometimes you made exceptions. Long before anybody I knew, you had Gorbachev on your radar and you predicted he was going to bring revolutionary and healthy changes to Russia and to the West. You admired Gurdjieff and resonated deeply with the masters of Zen and Sufi. You brought out the gold in Jesus' teachings and threw out the distortions. You knew so many masters from all traditions and treated them as your colleagues. You encouraged us to go to listen to another great Indian mystic, Krishnamurti — a playful acknowledgment from one guru to the anti-guru. I have always loved both of you and always will.

And still... sometimes I felt insecure, not knowing whether you were my teacher, or even a true teacher. Who was I to know? Those were heartrending moments.

But now, more than forty years after we first met, my gratitude towards you runs deeper than ever. You set me free.

Primarily you taught me to be full of joy again. As a child, I felt the postwar pain of my parents and grandparents. Even so, I was basically a carefree and happy child. After years of hard study, partly trying to earn my parents' love, that joy had become stuck.

How did I first hear of Osho?

After my 27th birthday I went with my girlfriend Nelly on vacation to France. We visited two dear friends who had bought a small and simple farmhouse in a remote area of Auvergne. They had just returned from Pune, India, where they stayed in an ashram. They were full and overflowing about their experiences there.

The four of us had a few idyllic days. I had successfully defended my doctorate, had obtained tenure, and was on my way to New York University to immerse myself in a very creative postdoctoral program. I was completely relaxed, in a *liminal* or in-between time. For a while, there would be no pressures on me, no worries.

My friends who had been in India loaned me a book about tantra from their teacher, Osho. It was called *Tantra, the Supreme Understanding,* and it is a commentary on the *Song of Mahamudra* by Tilopa, an Indian mystic from the 10th century. It spoke so directly to me that I could not put it down. I was sad to leave my friends and their hermitage as Nelly and I continued our travels to the Festival of Avignon.

The next day we stayed in Clermont-Ferrand and went to visit the cathedral. I started meditating, and a few minutes later it felt as if my body was dissolving in an enormous and frightening openness. I had no control over what was taking place. There was also a strange psychic awareness of the stream of thoughts of the people around me.

In the midst of all this, a crystal-clear insight bubbled to the surface — my life was going to take a very unexpected turn. It announced itself as a *knowing*, something beyond any discussion or argument, and I was shaken by its force. I also clearly saw that academia could not possibly be my final destiny. Still, it took seven more years before I would resign from my position of my own volition. This turning point in my life would unburden and liberate me.

The full blast and intensity of my cathedral experience lasted for about half an hour. Afterwards, my body needed more than twelve hours to shrink back to its accustomed "format." This process was very uncomfortable. The *knowing* present during this revelatory experience has never left me since. It is still with me now as I am writing down this memory.

Three years later, in the utmost secrecy, during the long summer recess, I became a disciple of Osho. My cathedral experience in Clermont-Ferrand had changed me and intensified my search for a teacher. The Indian mystic J. Krishnamurti and the Tibetan lama Trungpa attracted me very strongly, but after a long inward struggle my heart went with Osho. Just after I made my travel arrangements to go to India to meet him, he left for the U.S. and it was not clear initially where he would end up. Now that I was finally ready to go deeper, I could not wait any longer. I travelled to Amsterdam where one of his close Dutch disciples, Ma Arup, was giving initiations at the Osho center on a houseboat, during a big summer festival. After the initiations, there was a party that lasted all night long. I ended up fainting during this party, but not because of alcohol — I was literally intoxicated by the love energy in the air.

In two months I received my new name from Osho, based on my picture and an intake form, but then had to wait for another long year before I would be in his physical presence in Oregon, where a big community was forming.

I had not dared to disclose my intentions to become an Osho follower to any of my colleagues. This was, after all, no small potatoes. Outwardly, after having received my new name as Swami Deva Krishna, it was presumed that I would wear the orange sannyasin colors and a long mala of prayer beads, with a small locket of Osho's face at the level of the heart. For me, all that went against the grain of my conditioning. I understood what it meant and I planned to comply, but I was quite preoccupied wondering what people would think.

My biggest fear and challenge would be my first meeting of the school year with my Ph.D. supervisor, professor Carlos Tindemans. How would he react? He was an authority figure and could be quite judgmental. Though I liked him and was impressed by his academic achievements, I felt intimidated by him. It did not help that his brother Leo was a famous statesman, had been the prime minister of Belgium, and was a major player in European politics.

As part of my inward preparation and integration after my initiation as a disciple of Osho, I completed a weeklong, silent Vipassana meditation at an abbey close to my home town. The week was both fantastic and difficult. It was led by a very competent and loving Osho disciple who had studied with the brilliant

Advaita teacher, Nisargadatta Maharaj. My brother Filip was sitting next to me during the long hours of silence. Sometimes my mind became very still and I was in peace. Sometimes my mind was louder than ever, obsessively repeating, *What is Carlos Tindemans going to think when he sees me?* This concern hung over me like a dark cloud.

When I did meet Carlos in the university corridor, I felt too timid to give him an explanation. There I was, in my new orange garb with a little picture of a laughing man dangling around my neck. And Carlos — or so I thought — was too astonished to say anything. And he never did. You might imagine how psychologically taxing it was for both of us. After that, things were never quite the same between us. Maybe I had crossed, or even violated, some unspoken academic or cultural boundary.

With even greater anxiety I was anticipating my first public appearance in Antwerp. There was a theatre festival taking place in the central marketplace, and I knew I was bound to see some people from my past there. Would they even *recognize* me — Frank — who had suddenly morphed into Swami Deva Krishna?

I asked my two best friends to accompany me for support. Sure enough, right away my biggest fear manifested itself. Somebody I knew from the theatre world *did* recognize me and came towards me, totally convinced that I was playing a prank — the joke being that I was dressed as an Osho follower for this occasion. When I tried to make clear that I really was with Osho now, she couldn't stop laughing. She was sure I was still playing my part.

I knew full well that Osho was playing a clever trick, testing my self-conscious personality. My soul essence was willing to go through this, knowing that ultimately it would help me to be more myself, but my personality bristled with resistance. What a learning process, every single day! I had to continually either choose what I really wanted, or stay in fear of what people might think of me. It was often hard and painful, and quite tough on my parents too. Luckily there were the moments of delight. Now that I was *showing my colors,* I made many new friendships. Some, like Kathy, would last a lifetime.

Finally, I was able to be with Osho himself when I lived two years at "the Ranch," the community in Oregon, also known as Rajneeshpuram. I worked for one year at its beautiful organic farm and for another in its bustling kitchen.

The joy emanating from Osho was truly infectious. He was a spirited and inspiring speaker and he was able to elaborate deeply, playfully and effortlessly about all the religious and spiritual paths.

He certainly was a genius trickster. One day there was an announcement: Osho had released a list of 22 resident disciples who had reached a state of "enlightenment." I knew more than half of them, some of them quite well. The leader of the farm, Swami Neehar, an organic farmer from Australia, was on the list, and I was very fond of him. For about ten days the energy in the commune was highly electric. There was even an interview in the community's weekly newspaper and, of course, a lot of gossip. Neehar told me that when he heard he was on the list, something finally relaxed in him — a sense of having arrived.

Some jealousy quickly developed between some who had made the list and those who did not. Apparently, only one of the 22, and old disciple from India, wrote a funny note to Osho telling him that he was not fooled by his master and the bogus list.

Osho was certainly a role model for me, as someone who had quit his job at the university to totally dedicate himself to his spiritual mission. Each new generation is still discovering and devouring his numerous books. You can find the Osho Zen Tarot deck, based on Osho stories or insights, everywhere. My editor, Cher, tells me that this is the only tarot deck she owns, and that she often pulls a card for the day and leaves it on her desk. Also, YouTube has thousands of Osho videoclips. His joy in life has been captured for the future.

Around Osho, everything was always being celebrated. He often called laughter the heart of true religion. He encouraged us to live totally, passionately and intensely. I fondly remember what it was like being in the community around him in Oregon. Thousands of seekers from all over the globe came together with a common purpose — to allow for a new and healthier way of living together, based on love and the celebration of life.

Of course, there were also shadow aspects in this community — some rather shocking. There was certainly misuse of power, and some of it directly enacted by Osho's notorious and flamboyant secretary, Ma Anand Sheela, and a small group of disciples under her influence. Even before all this happened, I had my own energetic encounter with her. This took place in the midst of my personal crisis around whether Osho was an authentic teacher for me.

One day she came to visit the Osho community in Louvain, Belgium, where I was living at the time. I was curious to see her up close. At some point, she called the Osho headquarters in Oregon and we could overhear her conversation. I do not remember exactly was she was talking about, but I had a sinking feeling in my gut that it did not sound right. I kept watching her intently and, according to some of my friends, she seemed to be keeping a watch on me too. I evaluated her as being quite phony. The next day I left the community with tears and lots of self-doubt. I was down on myself, wondering if I just was not able to surrender to Osho.

The period that followed was one of the darkest in my spiritual life. In an attempt to get out of this impasse I decided to go back one more time to the big community in Oregon and be in the physical presence of the master again. Maybe my issue was with Sheela and not with Osho. This turned out to be the case. Later, it became clear that Sheela was involved in her own power politics. In retrospect, I learned to trust my intuition about what feels good and what feels fishy.

The day after Sheela left Oregon (and Osho) with the weird idea to start her own commune in Germany, I was awarded the gift of greeting him as he entered the meditation hall. This was not by accident. Some friends of mine knew about my misgivings about Sheela and had arranged this for me as a present. As I looked into the depth of his amazing eyes, there was not a trace of worry in him. In his lecture that day, he publicly revealed Sheela's betrayal and the psychology behind it. Ultimately, it would result in the unravelling of the community. Osho returned to India where he would once again begin a new phase of his work, this time delivering lecture after lecture on Zen.

For many years I would wolf down Osho books; I could simply not get enough of them. I have listened to so many of his lectures, some of them again and again. From that overflowing source, I would like to share now an early commentary he gave on the Upanishads, ancient Hindu philosophical texts written in Sanskrit. The Upanishads came into existence almost 5,000 years ago. Just as in Osho's teachings, there is no self-denial here. They are full of a vision in which we live in the world, play in the world and enjoy life.

Osho claims that his approach is close to that of the world of the Upanishads — that he was actually trying for the spirit of the Upanishads to be reborn in the world of today. They all were written as a form of poetry. One of them, the *Akshi Upanishad*, ends with the word *mystery*. Osho recommends taking the *mystery* into our heart every day.

In his book *Vedanta: Seven Steps to Samadhi – Talks on the Akshi Upanishad*, he indicates seven steps or phases. During the first three, effort is needed, but during the next three, effort is a hindrance. In the final phase there is transcendence. Nothing is needed anymore — no effort, nor the awareness to give up effort. Both are let go.

When Osho speaks about steps, he makes it clear that these "steps" only have a workable, utilitarian character and are not existential. Life is one and cannot be divided. These stages are not to be taken dogmatically or literally. Once we have understood what the search is all about, we forget about divisions and see that there is one progression, one flow.

I summarize the steps:

1. *For the seeker of truth, it is important to start from the heart and the feelings. As a seeker, you create an atmosphere around yourself in which the ocean is real and the waves are surface phenomena.*
2. *The second phase is about compulsive thinking. The seeker has to become aware of this and to be able to sometimes switch off the internal chatter.*
3. *In the third phase, you become the witness who is alert and is no longer attached to something.*
4. *In the fourth step, you see that there is only unity. The clouds have disappeared; only the sky exists.*
5. *In the fifth phase there is only truth. Worldly desires are no longer arising.*
6. *In phase six, all doubts have evaporated. Before it was still necessary to trust. Now this is also gone, but not because answers have come. Consciousness has simply shifted.*
7. *The seventh step is not a step at all. The seventh is you who have stepped through the phases. You have arrived in your true nature, as what you really are. There was never a time when you were not, and there never will be a time that you will not be. You will always be — you are not in time. The temporal can be defined in time. The non-temporal cannot be defined. It is timeless. Just as you are timeless, you are also spaceless.*

Opening to Love

When you are opening to love
you are riding a mighty wave
that is wanting and totally able to take you home.

It is your soul essence that immediately recognizes what home is.

It is not a foreign place.
It is very familiar.

Even as a kid you had a sense of this.
Can you still remember this?

A glimpse of a reality so nourishing,
so benevolent, so completely natural.

You are not remembering this in nostalgia.
You are contacting an inner reality.

When you contact something innocently,
with openness and depth,
it fuses with you.
It becomes yours.

Beings of immense compassion inhabit these inner realms.
They remind you constantly of your true nature.

The peace you experience here is the proof
that this is your real home.

7.7.1994.

CHAPTER 7.

CHÖGYAM TRUNGPA — Innate Goodness

ONE NEVER KNEW EXACTLY when Trungpa would make his entry. He could be a half hour or two hours late, as if lateness was not a concept to him. I had no problem with this, nor did I experience it as arrogance. For me, it was as if clock time had been put on hold. Linear time was being exchanged for cosmic time, during which events start when their time has come.

Usually, we students would all be cozily chatting together until he arrived. The moment he came in, I could sense something opening up in my consciousness, and I was ready to receive his brilliant insights.

I met Tibetan Buddhist teacher Chögyam Trungpa (1940–1987) at the Naropa Institute in Boulder, Colorado, which he founded in 1974. The Belgian National Foundation for Scientific Research had awarded me a wonderful opportunity: a grant to study there.

Naropa started out as a simple summer school. Only two or three hundred students were expected to attend, but to everyone's big surprise, 1,800 students enrolled. Something on a much larger scale was obviously afoot.

During the very first session in 1974, Ram Dass agreed to be the main speaker, along with Trungpa. Soon, many other well-known teachers and artists would come to inspire the students: Joseph Goldstein, Jack Kornfield, Rabbi Zalman Schachter, Allen Ginsberg, Williams Burroughs...

Trungpa radiated a magnetic and profound quality of "being," and many spiritual giants in their own right did recognize that immediately and wanted to be in his company. Thomas Merton, American mystic, priest and writer, met Trungpa in India in 1968, a short time before his unexpected death. He commented in his journal, "*Chögyam Trungpa is a completely marvelous person. Young, natural, without front or artifice, deep, awake, wise.*" (Mukpo)

Trungpa and Suzuki Roshi, founder of the San Francisco Zen Center, also established an immediate bond. Suzuki Roshi referred to Trungpa as being like a son, and gave explicit permission to many of his students to go study with Trungpa. Both Suzuki and Trungpa grappled with the monumental task they had taken upon themselves — working with the neurotic aspects of their students and of the world.

When Trungpa heard that Suzuki had been diagnosed with stomach cancer, he wept so intensely that a blood vessel in his eye burst, and blood-reddened tears flowed down his cheeks (Midal). Suzuki Roshi's inspiration partly led to the foundation of the Naropa Institute.

The Naropa Institute later morphed into Naropa University and obtained full academic accreditation. Since its inception, thousands of psychotherapists, psychologists and psychiatrists have been working with the psychological insights and clarity of Trungpa. He would discuss the various strategies or impulses with which the ego relates to its projections: indifference, passion and aggression. He would point out how

Thoughts form ego's army and are constantly in motion, constantly busy. Our thoughts are neurotic in the sense that they are irregular, changing direction all the time and overlapping one another. We continually jump from one thought to the next, from spiritual thoughts to sexual fantasies to money matters to domestic thoughts and so on. (The Myth of Freedom)

Trungpa's vision was never to establish a sectarian Tibetan Buddhist Institute, but to create a platform where all the wisdom traditions of the world would have a voice: to be genuinely alive and in dialogue with each other.

Never before had I experienced an academic institution so brimming with creativity and spirituality, or with such exceptional professors. I was amazed and impressed by the heartfelt interactions between teachers and students. This was most apparent in a psychology class I took in which the tantric discipline of relating to life was based on "the five buddha families." Each family is associated with a "neurotic" and an "enlightened" style. For the benefit of the students, the teacher would adopt different teaching styles, and was not shy to borrow tricks from colleagues teaching in the theater department. It was for the student to figure out whether he was acting out the "neurotic" or the "enlightened" style.

For example, one of the buddha families is called "Padma" (lotus flower). Padma neurosis is connected with unbridled passion, a grasping quality and a desire to possess. It is connected with the element of fire and the color red. In the confused state, fire does not distinguish among the things it grasps, burns and destroys. But in the awakened state, the heat of passion is transmuted into the warmth of compassion.

After experiencing such incredible warmth of compassion in action, I felt a very strong urge to connect the world of knowledge and information with meditation. After I returned from Naropa to my own department of Germanic Languages at the University of Antwerp, I immediately added a new elective course to my department. I called it *Non-Verbal Communication*, which was a way to smuggle meditation and mindfulness into the curriculum. Instead of the usual 9:30 a.m. time to begin the lectures, my students and I started at 6 a.m. Everyone took notice of how, on that particular day of the week, the students in this class were much more alert and vital than usual. And so was I!

I will always remember the cosmic presence of Trungpa, and I still get chills when I read about his passing and the goodbye ceremony that took place about seven weeks after his death. His wife, Diana Mukpo, has testified that being married to Trungpa was sometimes like being married to a cosmic force rather than a human being. She had been skeptical about the rumors that when a very realized lama dies, the heart remains warm for several days as the teacher remains in a state of *samadhi* (meditative absorption). She and others noticed that for three days, Trungpa's heart center did stay warm, and that there was no rigor mortis. The state of samadhi continued for five days. In Tibetan Buddhism, it is held that after the outer signs of life have ceased, the consciousness goes through a number of stages of dissolving into itself. Many old friends arrived from around the world, and people kept sitting around Trungpa's body in meditation and could still feel his cosmic presence.

Seven weeks later, over three thousand people attended the cremation ceremony. The fire puja was led by Dilgo Khyentse Rinpoche. When the fire began to die down at the end of the afternoon, there was a succession of rainbows in the sky. One rainbow encircled the sun while three hawks (some say eagles) circled and circled. A white cloud in the shape of an *Ashe* — a Tibetan symbol that expresses the open space of mind before the first thought — appeared.

For a long time, Trungpa had looked for a symbol that expresses enlightenment. All he knew was that it was black and monolithic. In 1976 he received it. After a long and intense night, at dawn, he asked for a brush, ink, and paper. He then produced a stroke of extraordinary power. The practice of *Ashe* became quite important in the community around Trungpa. *Ashe* is a great blade that cuts through all confusion, hesitation and fear and liberates the energy of basic goodness.

Ashe is also called the stroke of confidence. It is a form of calligraphy specifically developed by Trungpa to experience the essence of sacred warriorship, and is connected to the pre-Buddhist cultural tradition of Shambhala, an ancient kingdom. In seminars, students would sometimes execute the one stroke in turn while standing in a large circle. In the Shambhala vision Trungpa received, the warrior is a man or a woman who acts in the world with gentleness, fearlessness, and precision in order to overcome aggression and help others.

When the stroke is done wholeheartedly, there is no more a sense of a separate self. First, one takes time to feel strongly the solid earth under one's feet. Then one connects with the energy of space around and above. The blank sheet of paper symbolizes the open sky and an open mind and heart — open to all possibilities. One waits to make a first connection with reality — first thought. As the stroke is executed, it cuts through conceptual thinking, confused emotions and joins the mind and the body in a fresh way. As each person does one stroke, a strong life-force energy called "windhorse" is aroused.

Trungpa was so obviously fearless, and completely embodied the innate goodness he taught. Jeremy Hayward, one of his students, recounts the following anecdote. He was told that Trungpa returned to his house just after Jeremy had exploded at him. Trungpa expressed tremendous delight, probably because Jeremy had let down his barrier of politeness with him. He exclaimed, "Oh, Jeremy was *really* angry!" Then and there, he sat down and wrote a poem which was delivered to Jeremy the next day:

For Jeremy
Failing to be a grain of sand
Venom, nectar of a power maniac
Trying to catch that
Brings loss of this.
Avalokiteshvara's compassion has a smile.
Buddha is said to be humble
A follower of his is joyful
Let us be a smiling grain of sand.
Maybe with cow shit on the head.

Underneath it Trungpa drew a little flower, the words "Love" and "Loving" and his signature. (Hayward)

I had eagerly devoured some of his books before my visit, and I still think that he has left us some superb formulations of what mindfulness is all about. In his masterpiece, *Cutting through Spiritual Materialism* (1973), he analyzes how materialism is conquering the world, even in the realm of spirituality. Under the pretext of spiritual development, there is a tendency to give in to egocentric behavior: "*... to see spirituality as a process of self-improvement — the impulse to develop and refine the ego when the ego is, by nature, essentially empty.*"

Like the Dalai Lama, Trungpa escaped from the cruel yoke of the Chinese in Tibet just in time. He was then only 19. In his autobiographical *Born in Tibet* (1966), he describes his rigorous education as a lama after he was recognized as a reincarnation of an important teacher. When he was barely 18 months old, his parents had to let him go to be taken to an abbey. His official training started when he was five. Later he recounted that he could distinctly remember events from the early life of the tenth Trungpa, his predecessor.

When news spread in Tibet that Trungpa was fleeing to India to escape from the Chinese, many monks joined him. From a small group of less than a dozen, they quickly grew to three hundred. Their journey was harrowing — the hunger was absolutely brutal. They boiled leather footwear so they could drink something with nutritional value. After ten months they did reach the frontier with India — but only nineteen of them survived.

Amazingly, Trungpa, like the Dalai Lama, was never bitter or revengeful about this. As a spiritual warrior, he used all the hardships and deprivations to delve even more deeply into the quality of compassion. An excitingly hopeful and refreshing ambiance emanated from Trungpa himself. Compared to what he went through, every obstacle on my own journey seemed terribly insignificant.

While at Naropa, I was privileged to witness a moving meeting between Trungpa and the Dalai Lama on a stage in a big auditorium in Boulder. Apparently, they had not seen each other in quite a while. When they greeted each other, it was as if the warm glow of their hearts filled up the whole space. Here they were, two great Buddhist and universal grandmasters, each with their unique style of expression. They were both surprised to discover how deeply the people they met in the West were tortured by feelings of guilt, shame and self-deprecation. The "New World" was ready for a fresh transmission from the East. Unbeknownst to them, as they were fleeing from Tibet, many people in the West were longing for and waiting to receive this from them.

Trungpa refers to the essence of human nature as *basic goodness*. Sometimes it is also called *Buddha nature*. This does not mean that all people would be morally good — rather, it points to our original nature. Even when somebody is severely psychologically wounded, their intrinsic or innate goodness is still present (somewhere in there!). At Naropa, every person committed to a meditation practice every single day. When Trungpa was asked about the difference between meditation and psychotherapy, he responded that the difference is in the expectation one brings to these.

In the common psychological therapeutic modality, the client tries to surmount a particular difficulty. One is looking for a technique or method to solve or surpass one's problem(s). Meditation is an invitation to see and to accept that you are what you are. What you really are is sacred and does not need healing.

Today, the collected works of Trungpa, including his talks everywhere across the U.S., are readily available. Many people are still discovering him through the books and activities of his American student, Pema Chödrön (1936–). Millions all over the world celebrate her as one of the most beloved and insightful Buddhist teachers.

I love the depth in all of Pema's writings. The titles of her books, like *Comfortable with Uncertainty* or *The Places that Scare You,* reflect the approach of her teacher Trungpa, as well as seeming appropriate for the current climate we live in. I also like *Start Where You Are* and *When Things Fall Apart.*

Recently Pema's granddaughter was admitted as a student to Naropa University. Her grandmother promised her that she would speak at the opening ceremony. Again, Pema chose an interesting title for her lecture: *Fail, Fail Again, Fail Better,* alluding to the words of the Irish Nobel Prize winner for literature, Samuel Beckett. Pema explains how seductive and dangerous it is to consider oneself a failure when something goes wrong.

Pema knows what she is talking about. She felt herself to be a miserable failure when her second marriage went on the rocks. But the resulting depression led her to finding her teacher Trungpa. Many years later — when she was struggling with chronic fatigue and a painful back — it was again very tempting to let feelings of failure entangle her. With *Fail, Fail Again,* Pema means that it is inevitable that we will experience events that we do not want to happen. A negative self-image such as "I am a failure" will never remedy that. Neither will reproaching others for our own feelings.

It is so much more efficient to investigate — with curiosity — what is really at stake. Most of the time we have no idea where the investigation may lead.

What does Pema mean with *Fail Better*? Failure can open up an unprotected, vulnerable and very free space inside of ourselves. From such a space it is possible that the very best will come to the surface.

My fondest memories are about Trungpa as a formidable meditation master. After I participated with him in a retreat high up in the Rockies, something deepened in me that never completely left me. With Trungpa, we meditated with our eyes open, facing a central shrine on which he was sitting. He taught us to "go out with the outbreath" and then to allow for a gap. The inbreath should not receive any emphasis as it happens naturally anyway. In this way it was easy to become very expansive. As I was practicing I would often merge with the environment and when my eyes fell on Trungpa, I would see — and sometimes become — a mysterious, gigantic and inscrutable dragon. Really!

Today I can state with certainty that the flame jumping from teacher to student is a reality. I experienced this multiple times during a recent trip to Bhutan in December 2017. I could feel the presence of Trungpa in so many places! Bhutan is a wondrous kingdom situated on the ancient Silk Road between Tibet, India and China, and has a distinct national identity based on Buddhism. I had the unique opportunity to travel throughout Bhutan under the guidance of Ian Graham, whose grandfather had lived there for more than fifty years and founded the famous Dr. Graham's Homes (a residential school for poor and orphaned children) in 1900. The current and the former prime ministers of Bhutan are alumni of this educational system.

Bhutan occupies a special place in the life and in the teachings of Trungpa. In 1968, he went to Bhutan at the invitation of the queen, who was a very committed Buddhist practitioner.

They were both students of the well-known teacher Dilgo Khyentse Rinpoche, who also taught the Dalai Lama. While Trungpa was living in Oxford, he tutored Jigme Singye Wangchuck, her eldest son, who became king of Bhutan from 1972 to 2006.

In addition, Trungpa received permission to do a private meditation retreat at Taktsang, a famous cave where the 8th century Indian tantric and shamanic master Padmasambhava meditated before entering Tibet. He was the most important figure in the transmission of Buddhism from India to Tibet.

Trungpa was considered to be a "tertön", which in Tibetan means a "treasure revealer." As a young lama in Tibet, he had already discovered some hidden teachings. Now, during this retreat, it was the first time he was back in the region he was from. When he lived in Tibet, and then in India, and later in Britain, he experienced deep frustration over what he observed to be corruption of true spirituality. One night, sitting in this cave, a profound spiritual inspiration came through, during which he received a hidden text from Padmasambhava.

Five years later, now living in the U.S. and observing the spiritual scene, he published *Cutting through Spiritual Materialism.* Here Trungpa would work out these insights. He distinguishes three aspects of materialism, which he calls the three lords of materialism that constantly deceive us.

- **The lord of form** refers to the neurotic pursuit of physical comfort, security, and pleasure.
- **The lord of speech** refers to the use of intellect in relating to our world, especially the use of concepts as filters to screen us from a direct perception of what is. The concepts are taken too seriously and are used as tools to solidify our world and ourselves. The most fully developed products of this tendency are ideologies, the systems of ideas that rationalize, justify, and sanctify our lives (such

as nationalism, communism, existentialism, Christianity, Buddhism).

- **The lord of mind** is the most sophisticated of the three. The lord of mind rules when we use spiritual and psychological disciplines as the means of maintaining our self-consciousness, of holding on to our sense of self. Drugs, yoga, prayer, meditation, trances, and various psychotherapies can be used in this way. Ego is able to convert everything to its own use, even spirituality.

Of the many insights Trungpa transmitted, I offer you my own selection.

- *The religion of the Buddha isn't necessary, particularly, but the disciplines that we have developed and learned from, over the span of 2500 years, are necessary.*
- *Enlightenment is having an honest relationship with ourselves.*
- *We can only love when we have first developed a tender relationship with ourselves.*
- *To look for a purpose is always to look elsewhere, away from the immediacy of Being. Being is something primordial, timeless, and yet immediately present. Being is not be found in anything other than the immediacy of the experience, yet it has a dimension of vast vision not present in the momentary, passing aspect of experience.*
- *The Shambhala teachings are founded on the premise that there is basic human wisdom that can help solve the world's problems. This wisdom does not belong to any one culture or religion, nor does it come from the West or the East. Rather, it is a tradition of human warriorship that has existed in many cultures at many times throughout history.*
- *Warriorship does not refer to making war on others. Aggression is the source of our problems, not the solution.*
- *Warriorship is the tradition of human bravery, or the tradition of fearlessness. With this attitude, there is constant bravery and constant openness.*

- *The guru is a master warrior who teaches the students as apprentice warriors.*
- *Having been highly and completely trained, then there is room for crazy wisdom. According to that logic, wisdom does not exactly go crazy, but on top of the basic logic or basic norm, craziness as higher sanity, higher power, or higher magic can exist.*
- *The terms "enlightenment" or "Buddha" or "awakening" imply a tremendous sharpness and precision, together with a feeling of space. We can experience this. This is not only a myth.*

Fear completely disappears

It is so beautiful
that you could consider the cosmos as a living organism
filled with intelligence and love,
constantly interacting with you as consciousness.

On earth the signs are crystal clear.
Now white buffalo and white whale are here.
Their innocence awakens your vision
and your innate goodness.

During ceremony and meditation
there is an intimacy in which your heart simply knows
it is always part of everything.

Fear completely disappears
as you surrender to this intimacy of the heart.

Trust the reality of your own experience.
Don't you feel so much better
whenever the heart is softening?

To find your place in daily life
it helps to know yourself
as the cosmic being that you are.

Healing the pain in the world

Love surrounds you, always.
Deep, abiding love.

Knowing that love surrounds you
will eventually bring healing
to everything that was once broken in you.

If the lived, day-by-day, reality of love sometimes feels far away,
no worries — you can always call this reality closer to you,
whenever you want — why not now?

This is what you must discover —
in spite of betrayal, the innocence of your heart is still there
and can open and receive love.

In yet another discovery you will find
that when you treat the earth with respect
she becomes an ally and supports your awakening.

As the quiet in you is intensifying
you are getting ready
for the deepest discovery of all.
The perfection of your placement within the cosmos.

*In this place your love and peace are so profound
everything is being realigned into a sublime harmony.*

*Knowing yourself more and more consistently as love itself
is your way of healing the pain in the world.*

CHAPTER 8.

ECKHART TOLLE — The Now

THE FIRST TIME I sit in front of him, I know intuitively that Eckhart (1948–) will become a world teacher. He entered simply. Not necessarily shyly, but inconspicuously in a disarming and endearing kind of way. When you meet a vast being for the first time, there is a totally fresh and open impression that registers itself in the heart. At least this happens for me — with Osho, with Krishnamurti, with Trungpa and then with Eckhart. This most delicate and exquisite dance between the personality and the depth of being that infuses it, is revealed in a few seconds.

When I sit with Eckhart, I realize my blessings to be able to be, once again, in the presence of someone without a trace of an ego structure. During his talk he refers a few times to Ramana Maharshi, to Jesus and to Buddha. The rest of the audience is captivated too. We are in good company!

The talk takes place in a church in Portland, the city in the northwest of the U.S. where I have been living since 1986. His book *The Power of Now* has just been published. He is not very well known yet....

When Eckhart is finished — that night he talked non-stop for almost three hours in a deafening silence that emanates from him and reverberates through the audience — I can hardly contain my happiness. I like his message and I like the messenger. His delivery is refreshingly clear and sometimes hilariously funny. He is talking about the most serious issues facing humanity and he is also lighthearted about it, taking great delight in poking fun at the ego.

What Eckhart is saying resonates with the messages I have been receiving for many years. It confirms my trust that there is a new state of consciousness presently available on earth, and that it is very important to share and transmit this.

I will end up taking five retreats with Eckhart, including one in Santa Cruz that is specifically designed for professionals who help to spread his teachings. My qualifications: I had been using *The Power of Now* (when it was first translated into Dutch) as the manual for my workshop *Awakening to Love*, which I offered for many years in Belgium. Many of the *Inspired Guidances* included in this book came through there.

Another retreat in the early days with Eckhart took place at Breitenbush Hot Springs, one of my favorite spots on the planet. It is situated in the midst of ancient forests with revitalizing hot mineral springs. Indigenous people from all around the area used to gather there to sit in council and resolve intertribal issues. They would leave their weapons outside of the camp. The permanent community of about 50 to 70 people who live there now are completely off the grid. They make their own electricity via a dam on the Breitenbush River. Cell phones do not work at all on the property. I love to teach there and have done so for more than 25 years.

The weeklong retreat with Eckhart takes place in complete silence, except when he gives his talks. The camp is filled to capacity. There are one hundred attendees. Compared to the crowds Eckhart is drawing today, this is a very cozy, intimate setting. All of us have the opportunity to get a hug from him.

Later the retreat will be referred to as *The Rain Retreat* since it rains non-stop for six days. Eckhart jokes about it and tells us that if we were to surrender just a bit more the rain would stop. On the seventh day the sun is shining brilliantly in the open sky. When Eckhart comes out he just has to point his finger to the sky and everyone bursts out in great laughter.

It is really an amazing treat to receive a bath in the *now* in such a setting, with a committed group of people and Eckhart as our teacher. Kathy and I happen to be staying in a cabin next to Eckhart and his friend Kim Eng in the Breitenbush woods. I cannot remember ever sleeping more restfully. Soaking in the geothermal baths every day may have helped too!

Formed by my work with Grotowski and his associates, and after my discovery of Reiki, I started to include healing sessions in all my workshops. When I encountered Eckhart, I fell in love with his brilliant concept — the *pain-body.* I had experienced it for myself during my Osho days. For a solid year I practiced Osho's famous *dynamic meditation* daily. It was a year of letting go of pent-up pain and misery. Prior to doing this particular meditation, I was unaware of even having a *pain-body*!

Eckhart calls the remnants of painful emotions that have not been worked through the *pain-body.* Everyone has to deal with this; there is no escape from it. Even a newborn has it. This is so because the *pain-body* is not just individual but also collective. Humans are suffering because there is a collective memory of all the horrors that have taken place on our planet. Especially in relationships, one person's pain-body can activate another's. This painful and destructive dynamic can doom a relationship, as feelings of love may change to intense dislike or even hate.

Once I was teaching a small Reiki class of six women, and the class was going well. I liked everybody, they liked each other, and we were all having a great time. Yet, I could not sleep well during the class. Something seemed missing, still unresolved, but I had no clue what it was. I surrendered as best as I could to the process of the class. For some reason, towards the end of the class I started sharing about my birth, which had been surrounded by complications.

After I volunteered this information, five of the six women shared how extremely difficult their own birth process had been. It was quite incredible, and the healing that took place as a result of the sharing felt so very wholesome. I feel strongly that we had come together to help each other release our pain-bodies.

I do recommend, especially for younger people, trying out this *Osho dynamic meditation.* YouTube has many instruction videos — also, a CD called *OSHO Dynamic Meditation: music by Deuter* is a great help. The meditation lasts for about an hour and exists in five stages.

- The first one consists of very deep, rapid and chaotic breathing.
- In the second one, you allow yourself to *explode* in a conscious catharsis. You throw outside of you every tension that is ready to come out.
- In stage three you jump up and down with your arms raised while shouting the Sufi mantra *Hu-Hu-Hu.* Let the sound enter deeply into your sexual center. Exhaust yourself.
- STOP! The fourth stage is in total silence. You stand still in whatever position your body finds itself. You are witnessing every energetic change within.
- The last stage is dancing and celebrating.

Back to Eckhart — he points out that having insight into the origin and the functioning of the *pain-body* is a favorable condition for the flowering of consciousness.

I'd like to share an anecdote. For a while, it looked like the first four-day retreat I offered on *The Power of Now* might end in a disaster. Some of the participants were convinced that a rebellion was needed. This class did not have any content. Nothing was happening! I did not want to give up yet and felt very supported by Eckhart's example to patiently explain the difference between *doing* and *being*, again and again, with question and answer.

When I suggested to just rest into *being*, the immediate response was, predictably... *Yes, but how can I do this*? Sometimes it became quite hilarious. These days it is hard for most people to even imagine a state of non-doing. Luckily, *doing* and *being* do not have to be mutually exclusive. *Being — conscious being —* can be the deep, ever-present, undercurrent. Action arising from being is sustained and guided by the totality of existence.

I came up with a few helpful exercises. I asked the participants to tell each other, one-on-one, their life story. Each person had half an hour. One had the task to listen with attention and empathy, without intervening. The other was asked to tell his/her story in the third person — stream-of-consciousness style, with references to one's life path. For example: *When Marc was born as the sixth child to a poor family, just after World War II, he knew that he was not fully wanted. He was seven when his older sister died...* etc. This simple shift to the third person narrative resulted in a softness and compassionate understanding towards oneself and others which many had never experienced before.

Another exercise was an invitation to go for a silent walk into nature. Instead of walking through the woods, I suggested changing the perspective and to let the forest and trees *walk through them.*

After a few days of being together, the resistance to releasing mental thinking evaporated like snow in summer. In this metaphor, summer stands for *being* or the *now*. Tasting this is feeling an intense connectedness. Now, after more than a decade, I still sometimes meet with the participants of these workshops and we have a good laugh. How funny it really is to be in fierce resistance to the radiating reality of what is.

- *The ego mind is conditioned by the past and has brought the world to the brink of many disasters. Eckhart often calls the ego, "the imaginary me" or the "identification with mind."*
- *The Pain-Body consists of trapped life-energy that has split off from our total energy field and has temporarily become autonomous through the process of mind identification.*
- *The key is to be in a state of permanent connectedness with your inner body — to feel it at all times. This will rapidly deepen and transform your life. The more consciousness you direct into the inner body, the higher its vibrational frequency becomes.*
- *Silence is a potent carrier of presence, so when you read this, be aware of the silence between and underneath the words. Be aware of the gaps. To listen to the silence, wherever you are, is an easy and direct way of becoming present.*
- *Through allowing the "isness" of all things, a deeper dimension reveals itself to you as an abiding presence, an unchanging deep stillness, an uncaused joy beyond good and bad. This is the joy of Being, the peace of God.*
- *In his book* A New Earth, *Eckhart refers to the Sermon on the Mount where Jesus makes the prediction that the meek will inherit the earth. The meek are the egoless who have awakened to their essential true nature as consciousness and recognize that essence in all "others," all life-forms. This awakened consciousness is changing all aspects of life on our planet, including nature, because life on earth is inseparable from the human consciousness that interacts with it. In this way a new species is arising on the planet. You, who are reading and understanding this, at this very moment, are this new species!*

The present moment

Is there anything at all preventing you from being free,
right now, in the present moment?

Can you see that freedom is of the mind, and only of the mind?

Naturally, at the same time, you would choose for freedom
in all aspects of your life, whenever you can.

Getting stuck in the past or worrying about the future
is the opposite of freedom.

Without those mind activities
you are bringing the totality of your energy
into the exploration and celebration of the present moment.

Whenever this is happening all the forces of the entire cosmos
are at your side.

In these moments you are not a limited and separated entity.
You are experiencing the totality of your divinity.

Even your physical body becomes a divine body
when you just let it be in the present moment.

The present moment is not locked into time.
It stretches itself out indefinitely until it touches into eternity.

It is good to know that, no matter what, you are always free.

The sacred is right here.

Wherever you are, wherever you feel and look, wherever you breathe —
the sacred is right here.

When you keep this in mind you are naturally centered
and holding space for many.

Sharing sacred space is very joyful.

Your roots and the roots of the other are touching and strengthening.

It is a bit like leaving a sacred footprint wherever you are.

It is the sacred which manifests itself as your inner consciousness.

Your inner consciousness knows what you are and what you are here to do.

It participates fully in the realm of beingness.

This is the era of beingness.

Humanity is still so shockingly stuck in competing ideologies.

In beingness, everything arises organically, spontaneously,
perfectly and beautifully for the benefit of all beings.

You can see this, can't you?

You belong to a new wave of beings willing and able to ride this transformation.

Meditation, Reiki, yoga, Chi Gung, Aikido, shamanism
and many other spiritual disciplines are direct expressions of divine beingness.

The only goal is to deeply respect what you are,
what the other is and what the earth is.

Mutual respect and love are the hallmark of beingness.

Respect for diversity and uniqueness.

You are diverse and unique.

Beingness is always creating everything that is.

CHAPTER 9.

JESUS and A COURSE IN MIRACLES — The Miracle of Forgiving

AS MEISTER ECKHART PUTS it, *"God is at home; it is we who have gone for a walk."* I would say as much about my relationship with Jesus. I just could not find him when I was young. I had to go on a long walkabout before I became acquainted with him. The churches of my youth were somber, the priests uninspiring. The religious attitudes and behavior of my parents and grandparents were ambiguous and confusing. It was not until I met a French worker-priest when I was sixteen that I felt I was in the presence of a true Christian. And it was not until I was in my mid-thirties that Jesus finally became a true teacher for me. I could hear the Word as it speaks on every page of *A Course in Miracles*. He speaks to me often now, through my students and friends who share his love with me.

For me, studying and being with *A Course in Miracles* is healing my pain-body around the Jesus of my youth and the misunderstood Jesus on our planet.

It is well known that *A Course in Miracles* actually came into being when two people suddenly decided to unite around a common goal. Helen Schucman, Ph.D., and William (Bill) Thetford, Ph.D. were tenured professors in clinical psychology at Columbia University, New York, whose personalities often clashed. But in the Spring of 1965, Bill told Helen that he was fed up with the competition, anger and aggression that plagued their department. He was convinced that *there must be another way* and that he was determined to find it. Helen, for once, totally agreed with him and volunteered to help.

This triggered in Helen a series of remarkable inner visions that culminated in the figure of Jesus appearing to her both visually and auditorily. An inner voice would speak to her and say, "*This is a course in miracles, please take notes.*" Later, Helen referred to the seven years during which she would take down what she heard...

> *The Voice made no sound, but seemed to be giving me a kind of rapid, inner dictation which I took down in a shorthand notebook. The writing was never automatic. It could be interrupted at any time and later picked up again. It made obvious use of my educational background, interests and experience, but that was in matters of style rather than content. Certainly the subject matter itself was the last thing I would have expected to write about.*

A Course in Miracles is a self-study spiritual thought system. Its three-volume curriculum consists of a *Text*, a *Workbook for Students*, and a *Manual for Teachers*. It teaches that the way to universal love and peace — or remembering God — is by undoing guilt through forgiving oneself and others. Even though the language of the *Course* is that of traditional Christianity, it expresses a non-denominational, non-sectarian approach and sees itself as only one version of the universal curriculum, of which there are *many thousands.* At the end of the *Course*, the reader is delivered into the hands of his/her own inner teacher.

I love the succinct summary the *Course* gives of itself:

> *This course can be summed up very simply in this way:*
> *Nothing real can be threatened.*
> *Nothing unreal exists.*
> *Herein lies the peace of God.*

I can truly say that practicing and teaching the *Course* has helped me enormously in my life and in all my relationships. I must confess that I struggled through the *Workbook*, with its 365 lessons, no less than eight times. If truth be told, I can be a bit of a slow and headstrong learner. Whenever I came to Belgium to visit and teach, and my mom saw me lugging around this hefty tome, she would tease me and say, "Frank, when will you finally have finished reading this book?"

The other part of it is that listening to the voice and the teachings of the Jesus of the *Course* would carry me through many a situation. Moments of resistance would alternate with moments of spontaneous breakthroughs. This is still very much the case for me today.

A few years ago, in a residential teaching situation, I was absolutely appalled that one of my students — and actually me too — were being treated unfairly. I was about to walk away from it all, but first I went into nature to reflect on the situation. Sitting under a willow tree and feeling the pain in my heart, I asked myself, "What would Jesus do?" No sooner had I posed the question than a quote from the *Course* came to me: *"Do you prefer that you be right or happy?"* I was able to let my grievances go. It took some time, but love and forgiveness poured into the situation and resolved everything.

The *Course* aims to remove blocks to the awareness of love's presence. And Jesus poignantly says, *"The opposite of love is fear, but what is all-encompassing can have no opposite."*

The figure of Jesus presents itself quite differently from traditional Christianity. He does not see himself as someone who had to die on the cross to atone for our sins. He understands that his own apostles experienced a combination of sin, guilt and fear after the crucifixion. Jesus — in the *Course* — does not want his apostles to be martyrs, but rather to be teachers of peace and forgiveness.

Jesus takes the reader of the *Course* by the hand to learn the process and the miracle of forgiveness. The first step in this is the willingness to forgive oneself. Forgiveness is the means by which we remember our natural state. Through forgiveness, the thinking of the world is reversed. When we are succeeding in this, even with no more than a little willingness at first, we are able to open ourselves without judgment of others. Holding no one prisoner to guilt, we become free. Forgiveness liberates us from the prison of the past.

The first "publication" of *A Course in Miracles* (1333 pages!) appeared in the summer and fall of 1975, when 300 photo-offset copies were distributed to selected people. By now, 3 million copies have been sold, in 24 languages. In 1999 I heard that the Dutch translation was finally ready and would be presented to the public in Nijmegen, in the Netherlands. A team of 12 translators, including one colleague from my former University of Antwerp, had worked for 11 years to bring this to a satisfying end. It is a difficult linguistic challenge to do this. I decided to go, knowing that my time had come to start teaching the *Course* to my Dutch-speaking students for whom the English had been a barrier.

I vividly remember the panel discussion on that day, especially when Lulu Wang spoke. Wang is a Chinese-born writer who came to live in the Netherlands in 1986 at the age of 26 and has become a best-selling Dutch language author. As a kid, during the cultural revolution, she was in the Mao camps. In the middle of that gruesome "reality" ("brutality" would be a better word), she was able to survive psychologically by telling herself: *The world I am seeing here, cannot possibly be the real world.* It was quite a shock for her, living in the West, when she saw this very idea treated in-depth by Jesus in *A Course in Miracles.*

After they became "awake," both Eckhart Tolle and Byron Katie resonated immediately with the content of the *Course*, and still often refer to it. The goal of Jesus in the *Course*, in each sentence, in each paragraph, in each exercise, is to take us as fully as possible into the "Now."

I often mention to my students the remarkable vision Helen received a short time before the material started to come through. She saw herself entering a cave in a rock formation on a bleak, wind-swept seacoast. When Helen went to Israel several years later, she was startled to see that same seacoast at Qumran, where the Dead Sea Scrolls were discovered.

Her vision continued. She found a very old and large parchment scroll. She opened the scroll just enough to expose the center panel, on which only two words were written: "*God is.*" She slowly unrolled the scroll further, and tiny black letters began to appear on both side panels. The voice of Jesus explained the situation to her:

> *If you look at the left panel you will be able to read about everything that happened in the past. And if you look at the right panel you will be able to read about everything that will happen in the future.*

The little letters on the sides of the panel were becoming clearer, and for several minutes Helen was tempted to look at them. Then she made a firm decision. She rolled up the scroll to conceal everything except the center panel. The voice of Jesus sounded both reassured and reassuring. Helen was astonished at the depth of gratitude that it somehow conveyed. This time, apparently and finally, she had made the right choice.

I find one expression as the essence of the direct path. When one says, "God is," one can also say "Reality is" or "the Absolute is" or "Consciousness is." Rather that preoccupy oneself in thoughts about the past or the future, it is so freeing to see what is always there: the radiance of the Now.

In Part 1, I had briefly mentioned my visit to Qumran in 2009. Our group climbed on foot to the region of the caves where the Dead Sea Scrolls were found and meditated there for a while. At some point during our descent, away from tourists, I borrowed a shamanic hand drum from one of my students and did a spontaneous shamanization for our group. The sounds echoed back and forth between the mountains. It was very powerful and enchanting. Out of nowhere some tiny birds suddenly showed up and sang for us. For a moment the biblical past of the Holy Land merged into the timeless present. I felt close to the Essenes and to Jesus as a master teacher. Kathy, who does not care for heights, had stayed behind at the foot of the mountains and told us that she too could hear and feel the sound vibrations all the way down the valley and received a strong heart opening.

Jesus says

Give space, plenty of space to grace.

Your true nature is in a constant state of grace.

Grace and love are good companions.

Something inside of you already knows the way of love.
Trust that this is so.

Very patiently Jesus often explains
that God wants you to be happy, to be free, to be grateful.
Are you willing to choose for this?

Thousands of angels rejoice in your choice.

Jesus says: Use the Now to choose again.

If it looks like you are not willing to choose to be free
can you use your will to forgive yourself for this?

Connected to his loving will
your wondrous life unfolds.

God is. You are.

Relax now, gently and completely,
in the love you know you are.

When love is speaking to you
she touches you and changes you.

Jesus, as any great master,
could not care less whether you believe in him or not.
He would want to help you to be able to love yourself.

Jesus is as an older brother.
He has looked through the illusions of the world
and is now able to take you to source.
To the reality of what is.
Only if this is your wish.

He says, very simply, "God is. You are."

Creation is an eternal song of love.
Is it your will to hear this?

In God's plan for salvation
help is available to you
every step of the way.

1997. "le CHRIST: MON ROYAUM PAS d'ici!"

CHAPTER 10.

SRI AUROBINDO and THE MOTHER — Integral Yoga

SRI AUROBINDO AND "THE Mother" are inseparable in my view. When the Indian yogi Aurobindo met Mirra Alfassa, he called her The Mother, referring to the divine "Universal Mother." They were not a romantic couple, but two magnificent beings who worked together to boost the evolution of human consciousness.

When I first discovered writings from and about The Mother, I was riveted. I devoured thousands of pages of her occult and practical wisdom. I literally could not stop reading. It gave me a sense of real hope for humanity.

At exactly that time in my practice as a body worker, more and more clients would come in and share about their processes of transformation. I listened to their stories, their experiences and their bodies. I thought of The Mother and what she went through on her journey of bodily transformation. She would meet so much resistance that constantly arose from the subconscious. From her I would learn to be patient and very vigilant. She became my invisible helper, always by my side.

From the moment I became deeply interested in The Mother, she would regularly walk into my life, sometimes in a mysterious fashion. The very first time I was invited back to Belgium to offer my esoteric and shamanic sound work, I had an unusual experience with her energy. A few hours before the workshop was scheduled to start, I suddenly became unwell and feverish. I was wondering whether I would have to call off my event and debated what to do.

My hosts had an extensive spiritual library, and as I leafed through one of their books, a tiny picture of The Mother fell on the floor. I picked it up and looked at her, very intently, and I had an odd feeling—she was so alive in this picture, and gazing back at me, as if she were giving me darshan. Less than ten minutes later I was totally well, feeling incredibly invigorated and ready to go!

I have a little booklet at home called *Douce Mère (Sweet Mother),* in which the author interviews The Mother about the photographs that are taken of her. In it, she states that in general, those pictures capture "... one of my infinite states of Consciousness and various moods of expression caught eternally in one moment." Since that first "photo experience" with The Mother, I have had many more — usually not so dramatic, but delightfully subtle and uplifting.

Now, with the advantage of thirty years of hindsight, I have a deeper understanding of why she is so important both to my own development and also for humanity at large. This may seem over the top, and yet I believe that Mother has been able to open a door. I will elaborate on this in hopes that her project becomes clear to you.

Mother said:

> *What has happened, what is truly new, is that a new world is born, born, born! It is not the old world being transformed, it is a new world that is born! And we are right in the middle of the transitional period in which the two are still entangled in each other — when the old one still persists all-powerful and entirely dominating the ordinary consciousness, but when the new one is slipping in, still very modestly, unnoticed — unnoticed to the point that, for the time being, outwardly it doesn't disturb anything very much and that to the consciousness of most people it is even altogether imperceptible. And yet it is working, it is growing, till it will be strong enough to assert itself visibly... (Van Vrekhem, The Mother: The Story of Her Life)*

Mother was quite clear about her vision. She would found a city: the city of Auroville. It was part of her dream for the realization of human unity, with a new type of society that was balanced, just, harmonious and dynamic. Once she called Auroville the Tower of Babel in reverse. "*Then they came together, but separated during the construction; now they are coming again to unite during the construction.*" (The Mother, *Mother's Agenda*, September 1966)

What is Auroville?

Let us go back in time.

On February 28, 1968, near the town of Pondicherry in South India, representatives and youths from 124 countries and 23 Indian states gathered to support the utopian vision of The Mother. The Dalai Lama was there too, though Tibet was not independent at that time. They all brought a handful of earth from their region to put it in a large urn.

This is the official moment when Auroville, *City of the Dawn*, was founded, with the support of UNESCO. It will become one of the most exciting experiments of the 20th century, and it is still evolving.

It was very important to Mother that Auroville did *not* become yet another religion. She herself handwrote Auroville's charter in French. All of India Radio (AIR) broadcast the charter, live, in 16 languages. This charter was placed with the soil from all the represented countries and sealed in the urn, as a powerful message and promise:

1. *Auroville belongs to nobody in particular. Auroville belongs to humanity as a whole. But, to live in Auroville, one must be a willing servitor of the divine consciousness.*
2. *Auroville will be the place of an unending education, of constant progress, of a youth that never ages.*
3. *Auroville wants to be the bridge between the past and the future. Taking advantage of all discoveries from without and from within, Auroville will boldly spring towards future realizations.*
4. *Auroville will be a site of material and spiritual researches for a living embodiment of an actual human unity.*

When she was asked where exactly Auroville should arise, she used her pendulum and a map to find it. It pinpointed an ancient banyan tree in the middle of nowhere, about ten miles outside of Pondicherry, a small city on the Bay of Bengal in India.

The first Aurovilians faced many challenges. Many came and many left. They met with a climate of extremes —very hot summers with high humidity and intense monsoon rains. In this jungle, most elementary conveniences were still lacking. You had to share your habitat with cockroaches, rats and poisonous snakes, scorpions and ants. Initially this was hardly anyone's idea for a site of a new utopian community.

A lot has changed, as any visitor can see now with their own eyes. At this moment (2018), Auroville is a growing community of 2,400 people from 50 nations. Half of the inhabitants come from India. Artistic, spiritual and ecological experiments complement each other. It is possible to feel everywhere the presence of the Mother, who passed away five years after Auroville came into being.

When I was younger, I felt an intense sorrow that I never met Mother in the flesh. It could have happened; she left her body when I was 23.

But later, when I had the chance to sit several times in meditation in the Matrimandir (*The Temple of the Mother*) in Auroville, in South India, my sorrow completely disappeared. These meditations were beyond my wildest expectations, and the experiences became stronger each time I went. The Mother — and what she stands for — lives!

The Mother has said that since the beginning of the universe, the "Supreme" only had one design. It is to utilize all the energies towards one goal — that everything can find its soul. During my Matrimandir meditations, I could sense the truth of this vision: the presence of a vast, conscious, unifying power throbbing with an unimaginable transformative potential.

My greatest joy was to twice bring an international group of students and friends to Auroville and sit with them in the Matrimandir.

The first time I approached the Matrimandir, it evoked a memory of when I was eight. Our school went to the 1958 World Fair in Brussels and I was mesmerized by its iconic main pavilion, The Atomium (now a museum). I watched the sun illuminate its nine silver spheres, which represent the shape of an iron crystal.

By contrast, imagine the Matrimandir: an impressive golden globe rising from the earth into the sky. It is really a perfect symbol. Inside that globe, everything is sparkling and immaculately white. The sun's rays are projected into a large, perfect crystal in the main chamber. Twelve tall pillars rise towards the ceiling but do not quite touch it. On the marble floor is a beautiful white carpet. In the midst of noisy India, one enters an oasis of intense silence.

Mother had envisioned this temple, had actually *seen* it before it was built. This temple already existed *somewhere* but still had to be constructed in material form. The international team of architects around Mother argued with her that it could not possibly be achieved technically. Mother was adamant that it had to be. Why else would she be seeing it? It was characteristic for Mother never to give up...

The Matrimandir was finally finished in 2008, many years after her death, and is the spiritual and geographical center of Auroville — its living soul.

Who is The Mother? Who is this mysterious woman, and what role has she played? Could it be true that she, together with Sri Aurobindo, has given a decisive push forward to the evolution of human consciousness? I would like to make a case for this.

The best books (that I've found) written about The Mother are by the Flemish Belgian author Georges Van Vreckhem, a poet and artistic director of the official theatre company of Ghent, my home town. He made translations of the *Ramayana* and *Mahabharata*. He became acquainted with the work of The Mother in 1964 and moved to India in 1970. There he lived, in the Aurobindo ashram in Pondicherry and also in Auroville, till his death in 2012. His book *Beyond the Human Species, The Life and Work of Sri Aurobindo and the Mother* is a must-read. He was given free access to the rich archives of the ashram, including some of the private correspondence of Aurobindo and The Mother.

The Mother was born in 1878 in Paris as Mirra Alfassa. Her father was Turkish, her mother Egyptian. From a very young age, Mirra mixed and mingled with the world of the impressionist painters who were experimenting with the qualities of light. She knew Matisse and Auguste Rodin. The youngest of that whole group, she herself was a gifted artist. She was also friends with Alexandra David-Néel, the Belgian-French Buddhist explorer who was able to get into Llasa in Tibet at a time when this was still absolutely forbidden. She met Inayat Khan, the great Sufi musician, and was very close to `Abdu'l Baha´, the leader of the Baha'i movement, who built the Lotus Temple in New Delhi.

Mirra was always a remarkably gifted person. When she was five she was already aware of a special mission, and she practiced a form of meditation, although nobody taught her how to do this. She found this inner world so interesting that she preferred it even to visiting the circus with her father.

When Mirra was thirteen, for almost a year she would leave her physical body at night. Each time she was lying in bed, she would ascend, first above her house, and then high above Paris. She saw herself in a beautiful golden cloak, which was getting larger all the time, until it became as a protective roof above the whole city. She saw adults, children, and especially the sick flock together from everywhere to get underneath her cloak and beg for help. Then the cloak would expand even further and offer help to everyone individually. Nothing made young Mirra happier than these nightly escapades.

Even though she did not have a religious education, these experiences made it clear to her that it was possible to connect oneself in consciousness and be in action with something that can be called *the divine*. At the same time, during the sleep state, she received a practical discipline from different master teachers to accomplish all this. One of these masters became more prominent for her, and she would recognize him as Krishna. She knew that she would meet him one day on earth, and that it was with him that the divine work was to be done.

I often notice how meticulously and brilliantly the divine plan is doing its work. Just look at what was happening elsewhere at the same time...

Aurobindo Ghose was born in Calcutta in 1872, the third son of a Bengali doctor. At the age of seven, he and his two brothers were sent to England where he would remain until he was twenty. When he was eleven years old, he had a premonition that great revolutions were going to take place in the future and that he would have some role to play. He studied at the famed King's College in Cambridge where he became a classical scholar. Because of an inadequate financial allowance, he lived in severe poverty. In spite of this, he accomplished the dream of his father — he graduated at the head of his class with an English education.

In 1893, Aurobindo went back to India. When he put his feet on Indian soil, he had a sudden and remarkable religious experience of unity. 1893 is also the year that Vivekananda, disciple of Ramakrishna, sailed to the United States to share the light of the Vedanta.

Back in India, Aurobindo turned against the brutal and racist oppression of the British. Very soon they considered him as the *most dangerous man in India*. Aurobindo wanted to imprint freedom into the spirit of his people. He could write like no other, and he mastered 15 languages — some sources even say 17!

He was imprisoned by the British under false pretenses in 1908 and put into solitary confinement. The figure of Krishna appeared to him and assured him that everything would turn out well, and that he should apply himself to yoga. Aurobindo followed this advice and was able, in a very short time, to stop all compulsive thinking. What a feat! He had a whole slew of unity experiences, and he was recognized and treated as a king by his fellow prisoners and freedom fighters. If asked, they would gladly give their lives for him.

A year later, after a notorious trial, he was acquitted because of lack of evidence. He left in secret for Pondicherry, which was then a French enclave in India where the British could not bother him as much. He arrived there in 1910 and received shelter from local freedom fighters. A group of disciples gathered around him spontaneously. His influence was growing in this phase of his life, and he was known mostly as a very advanced yogi.

Even though India forever will remember him — together with Gandhi — as a great political leader and freedom fighter, he now applied himself to an inner, spiritual revolution. Mirra Alfassa met him in that capacity in 1914, just before the outbreak of the First World War. She immediately recognized him as the Krishna of her nightly adventures. After meeting Aurobindo, she lived for four years in Japan where she becomes friends with Rabindranath Tagore, the famous author and first Indian Nobel Prize winner. In 1920 she joined Aurobindo and never left India again.

Together, relentlessly, they developed the *integral yoga*, a method to integrate spirituality in daily life. This yoga is not an escape from life. On the contrary — all life is yoga! Yoga as a fundamental search for truth, for the meaning of life and a way to become completely human.

To surrender, to totally give of oneself, is the golden key concept of this yoga. "*In this Yoga nothing is too small not be utilized and nothing too big not to be tried out*," wrote Sri Aurobindo. And Mother said, "*Sincerity is the safeguard, it is the protection, it is the guide, and finally it is the transformative power*."

In India, there are traditionally three types of yoga. *Karma yoga* aims for a union with the divine through action or activities. The main example of this are the teachings of Krishna in the epic stories of the *Mahabharata*.

Jnana yoga is the way through knowledge and insight into the true reality. These are the Vedantic teachings Vivekananda took to the West. You will remember that Ramana Maharshi focused mostly on this.

Finally, there is *bhakti* yoga, which allows us to unite with the divine in a devotional way, for instance through the singing of mantras. Later we will see that Amma sometimes makes room for this in her worldwide events *(See Chapter 12)*.

Aurobindo and The Mother combined the essence of these three ways in their work, and further developed them into the *integral yoga*.

In 1927, Aurobindo retreated to his ashram room and dedicated himself exclusively to integral yoga. He ceded the practical leadership to Mother and entertained a massive correspondence with his disciples. After his death in 1950, Mother continued this laborious work on her own, pushing herself to the extreme. Her unique quest was an adventure into the unknown — how to change an ordinary human body into a supramental one? Luckily for us, her experiences have been preserved in daily recorded talks with Satprem, a French disciple. Step by step, she describes her bodily changes from the moment her cells began opening themselves to the *supramental consciousness.*

Aurobindo and Mother maintained that consciousness is the fundamental thing in existence. Humans are conscious of very little, and are usually *not* conscious of their own awareness. The mental consciousness of the human is not able to know reality. The supramental consciousness is much subtler and also more powerful. "*One might say the more truly concrete; it is less bound than the gross, it has a greater permanence in its being along with a greater potentiality, plasticity and range in its becoming.*" (Aurobindo, The Life Divine, p.257)

Mother applied all her yogic work to bring this consciousness into the earth's atmosphere, and the major breakthrough happened on February 29, 1956. It would later be called the "Golden Day."

Mother reports:

> *This evening the Divine Presence, concrete and material, was there present amongst you. I had a form of living gold bigger than the universe, and I was facing a huge and massive golden door which separated the world from the Divine. As I looked at the door, I knew and willed, in a single movement of consciousness, that 'the time has come,' and lifting with both hands a mighty golden hammer I struck one blow, one single blow on the door and the door*

was shattered to pieces. Then the supramental Light and Force and Consciousness rushed down upon earth in an uninterrupted flow. (Van Vrekhem, The Mother, The Story of Her Life pg. 415-425)

According to Aurobindo, the *Mother* concept stands for the big, evolutionary, conscious and intelligent principle of Life, of the Universal Mother. The Mother tries to lift humanity beyond its current limitations to its next step of evolution, which is called the *supramental consciousness*. Aurobindo and Mother saw that the supramental would manifest a decisive change in the earth's consciousness.

Aurobindo and The Mother employ a certain logic in their description of the stages of the manifestation of consciousness on earth. This perspective gives hope for both the earth and for humanity.

First comes the kingdom of the minerals, or so-called "inert matter." Then plants and flowers and trees appear, alive but unable to move around. Next the animals arrive, which are mobile, and then the humans, who possess a mental consciousness with which to dominate and rule. This is a huge and meaningful evolutionary leap. However, it creates many problems both for humans and for the earth, because humans are unable to calculate the consequences of their actions. In the vision of Aurobindo and Mother, they will accomplish this in the next evolutionary step—the phase they call *the supramental.*

Though Mother and Aurobindo were able to observe the hopeful changes in their own bodies and consciousness, they also became more acutely and painfully aware of all possible resistances coming from every side, even from those closest to them. Mother would often ask the people around her, *"Are you really ready for this great adventure?"*

She explained that everything that formerly was able to hide itself would be brought to the surface and into the light, by the supramental. More than forty years after Mother's death, we can see all of this so clearly on the level of politics and economics, in our climate situation, and in the world of finances and health care.

The greatest hope, but also the biggest challenge, is precisely *how* to allow this shift in consciousness. Many of the *Guidances* at the end of this book encourage us and point to how to do so. There is a quality of light that reverberates in them, and also a simplicity which touches the heart.

Not only is The Mother one of my constant masters, but also one of my guides. I will elaborate more on this notion of a guide in Part 4, Inspired Guidances, Chapter 1, "Guides and Angels of Light, Love and Peace."

I am fully aware that having a guide or guides can be very subjective. At the same time, as I experience reality, there is a very special and even familiar recognition of my own guides within. This is true for many people I know, and perhaps for millions of people on the planet. Aurobindo himself tells us briefly about an experience in his life:

> *I sometimes turned to the Gita for light when there was a question or a difficulty and usually received help or an answer from it. It is a fact that I was hearing constantly the voice of Vivekananda speaking to me for a fortnight in the jail in my solitary meditation and felt his presence. The voice spoke only on a special and limited but very important field of spiritual experience and it ceased as soon as it had finished saying all that it had to say on that subject. (Sri Aurobindo, Sri Aurobindo on Himself)*

Another anecdote from my own life:

Around Christmas of 2015, Kathy and I were back in Paris to participate in a series of dialogues with our favorite Advaita teacher, Francis Lucille. I was strongly drawn to a yoga center that I discovered very close to our hotel, but is seemed to be closed for the season. From outside it was hard to see what kind of yoga was practiced there. But I didn't give up, and on December 23rd I found the place open.

Its name is TAPOVAN, and it was founded in 1982 by Kiran Vyas. It turns out that Kiran had actually received darshan from Sri Aurobindo in 1948 at the tender age of four, which was most unusual and probably unique. Fifty years later, Kiran would talk about this publicly for the first time... "*When I left darshan, I understood the reason for my presence on earth.*"

I can empathize very well with what Kiran Vyas says here, because I myself am very sensitive to the energetic transmission taking place during *darshan*, a blessing by a spiritual leader. In Sanskrit, darshan means *to see* or *vision*. This ancient tradition is often used as a form of initiation in India. In the physical presence of someone like Sri Aurobindo, The Mother, Mother Meera or Amma, there is a transmission of subtle energies. The power of their seeing is such that one is able to *see clearly* as well, at least during the brief time of transmission.

Tapovan is a reference to a peaceful forest in ancient India where the sages practiced their yoga. As a boy, Kiran Vyas was educated in the international school of The Mother in Pondicherry, and he often had personal contact with her.

As I looked around the yoga center, I saw the French editions of Sri Aurobindo's and The Mother's works. I asked the shopkeeper if there were still massage appointments available that week and she told me that they had one, two days later. I thought to myself, *That is Christmas; this must be an error*. I double-checked with her — twice! — about the date, and it was twice confirmed.

So, there I was on Christmas Day, at 5 p.m. sharp. The center was obviously closed. I was about to walk back to my hotel when a car arrived and an Indian couple got out. They lived next to the center. I assumed there could be a connection with the center, and so I told them about my appointment. They assured me it

"le christ. résucité et deux stes. femmes"

must be a mistake — who would work on Christmas? Then the man negotiated for a moment with his wife and told me he'd be happy to offer me a massage there. I accepted and had an extremely delightful Ayurvedic massage. I also learned that he is the younger brother of Kiran Vyas and that his name was Pankaj.

Pankaj was obviously proud of his brother and deeply connected to The Mother. It was one of those moments where many threads in my own life were woven together to make a meaningful pattern. I was touched that Pankaj had spontaneously offered to spend part of his Christmas with me. As he massaged me, I could feel the presence of Mother in him, in the room and in me. What a great Christmas present from Mother!

The Mother loved to explain — as simply as possible — the difficult subject of integral yoga. She held conversations with the youth in the ashram about a variety of topics, always with a great sense of humor. She would cover art, war, religion, the real meaning of death, our transformation as part of evolution, and more. Here is a short selection to show how Mother was planting seeds in the minds of those young people.

- *Truth is not a dogma that one can learn once and for all and impose as a rule. Truth is infinite like the supreme Lord himself and it manifests at every moment in those who are sincere and attentive.*
- *There exists a level where all possibilities are present.*
- *One has to "become" what one wants to know.*
- *The role of the supramental is to transform the world.*
- *Only when the world will be transformed, will the Divine be able to express itself in its purity.*
- *There is nothing that is not God, but there can be chaos.*
- *There is a specific state of consciousness which corresponds with radical healing.*
- *Freedom and predestination, free will and determinism are truths belonging to different levels of consciousness.*
- *To be able to be divine, one has to be spontaneous.*
- *The first obligation of those who have responsibility for others, is to learn how to empathize with them.*

Divine Mother

Divine Mother is here and she wants to help.

Receive her blessings through the supramental light.

Let it penetrate in your heart and spread through all the cells of your body.

It removes obstacles, one by one.

It does so gently and very precisely.

To live in this light and as this light
is the great opportunity of your current incarnation.

All of nature is celebrating this light.

Accepting this light makes it more available to everyone around you.

When you are being challenged, do not despair.

The light is still there.

One insight.
One glimpse of light.
One receptive cell.
Grace is working.

Divine Mother has touched your heart.
From now on you are never apart.

Shalom!

Humanity in its current form cannot survive.
Have no fear.
This is rather a good thing.

Evolution and Nature are providing the solution.

In the new form it will be impossible to bypass the heart.

Through the work of Sri Aurobindo and The Mother
Divine Love has been able to penetrate very deeply
into the material structure of the Earth's atmosphere.

It is affecting everyone, knowingly or unknowingly.

It is a matter of cellular transformation of the human body.

It opens the way for consciousness to manifest itself much more directly.

Its effects in the world are very visible already.
It is like a shifting of tectonic plates.

The rigidity of the structures of patriarchy are being exposed
while the ascent of the Divine Feminine is unstoppable.

Your deep aspiration to no longer feed the problem
makes you part of the solution
and brings the new form into being.

Shalom!
Peace is possible
when Divine Feminine and Divine Masculine recognize and respect each other.

CHAPTER 11.

MOTHER MEERA — An Incarnation of the Divine Mother

Is it possible? Is there again an incarnation of the Divine Mother on earth? I wanted to know for sure, but it sounded too good to be true. In 1992, I found a small book by Mother Meera called *Answers* in the New Renaissance Bookshop, the popular New Age bookshop in Portland, my hometown. I always love to teach there.

In this little booklet, someone expressed the concern that people coming to see her might interfere with her work. Mother Meera simply answers: "Nothing can and nothing will interfere with my work. If the whole world came to me, my work would not be interrupted or deflected for a moment. I am working on all planes. I am working everywhere. This Earth is only one of the planes where I am working. How could anything disturb my work?"

Five months later, I was sitting silently in front of her. The procedure was the same for every visitor. She would be sitting on a chair, and when it was my turn, I knelt down close before her so her fingers could rest on my temples. I put my hands gently on her feet, which were covered by a beautiful sari. Her touch was precise, soft, strong and heavenly. I would feel it for hours afterwards. After 15 to 20 seconds, she released my head and I sat back on my heels. Now came the moment that I could look into her amazing eyes, and for a brief moment, I completely disappeared into them. A portal into the cosmos, into infinity.

For four consecutive days I was allowed to visit Mother Meera in her home in a tiny village in southern Germany. This was standard procedure for those who came to see her for the very first time. All in all, I have sat in front of her more than a hundred times — every single time I went to Europe, and later in the U.S. when she started to travel a lot. And I told all my students and friends about her and many would find their way to her. No one ever regretted it — on the contrary! Wondrous phenomena abound around her... plenty of synchronicities and deep healings on many levels.

Tommy is a dear friend who often came to sit with me in my home in the early days of the Inspired Guidance meditations. After hearing about my experiences with Mother Meera, he also became drawn to her. He knew he would never be able to travel to Germany to see her, so he prayed and asked her to please come to the United States. She had not really been traveling much at all, except to India. Then, within a month, she announced a U.S. tour. Tommy read that she was going to come to Seattle and San Francisco. So again, he prayed that she would come to Portland. Then Corvallis, about 50 miles away, was added to the tour. Tommy signed up immediately. To this day, almost ten years later, he is touched by the tenderness of the brief moment she looked in his eyes.

The night after he saw her, he had a vivid dream in which Mother Meera appeared to him. He was the only one in the room with her and she gave him the mantra "Aham Prema" (I Am Divine Love).

A friend had gifted Tommy with a beautiful golden box with Mother Meera's picture on it, wrapped with a golden ribbon, and filled with pencils embossed with the words "I am Divine Love." As he shared his Mother Meera story with our group, he offered each of us a pencil. We could all feel her presence in our room.

Rita and her partner, two of my Belgian Reiki students, went to visit Mother Meera at the same time I was there. Rita's biological clock was ticking away — she had been trying to get pregnant for a few years. Sitting in front of her, she silently expressed her deep wish to Mother Meera. For the briefest of moments, Mother Meera's gaze went to Rita's belly. A few people in our small company actually noticed this. After darshan we talked among ourselves and speculated about Rita's wish and our perceptions of what had transpired. Nine months later Yoni was born...

One summer, on the Fourth of July in 1999, Kathy and I were staying in our usual pension in Germany. We had become friends with our landlady Inge. Mother Meera had just moved her darshan venue to a bigger place, and Inge offered to drive us there. She also took Fred, a California guest who was staying with her and had come to see Mother Meera for the first time. On our way, just before turning right, Inge slammed on her brakes as a very fast driver — remember we are in Germany! — was speeding from the left. The car behind us bumped into us. Our car was totaled but still drivable. Kathy had a whiplash and for a brief moment I had absorbed the explosive energy of near-fatal danger. Even though Inge was in shock herself, she was still able to take us to our destination barely in time to see Mother Meera. Since we were so late, we were surprised to receive a front seat. It was an exceptionally strong darshan for Kathy, me and Fred. Inge, quite happily, was reimbursed by her insurance and got a brand new car...

The story is not finished. Naturally we got to know Fred quite well afterwards. When he heard we had been coming to Mother Meera for years, he humorously and grudgingly changed his mind-set — he had first hoped that one visit to her would suffice to change his life forever. So, on his next visit, he wrote Mother Meera a letter in which he specifically described what kind of partner he had been waiting for. Miraculously, he did meet that partner during that visit. Dagmar lived in Germany, and they came to live next door to us for a while in Portland. They took Reiki classes from me and we still are the best of friends. I performed their wedding close to Mother Meera's house. Two beautiful hawks came out of nowhere to participate. When the wedding pictures were developed, lights were clearly visible above the cemetery where Mother Meera's uncle, Mr. Reddy, had been laid to rest.

Mother Meera was born on Christmas Day, 1960, as Kamala Reddy in the South Indian village of Chandepalle. It was and still is a small village of a few thousand people. Her parents were illiterate farmers who owned a mango garden and rice fields. She spent most of her early childhood at the farm. Her family needed their six children to work, and therefore she and her siblings were initially not taught to read or write.

During harvest time, her generous parents allowed people to take food as they needed it. Mother Meera says she had a happy childhood even though she was not terribly close to her family. She knew early on that she was different. Her mother knew this as well. Even though she was smaller than the other kids her age, she felt like an elder person whose duty was to protect them.

On occasion, she was afflicted with strange physical symptoms, such as fainting spells and high fevers. She was independent and fearless, introverted, and drawn into silence. She would wander into the forest at night by herself, going alone from one farm to further ones. She felt she was not alone, that there was always "Somebody" with her. She was never afraid of the snakes she met, and because she was calm, they stayed calm.

Shortly after her sixth birthday she seemed to lose consciousness for an entire day. This was her first full immersion in Samadhi, as she later shared with her uncle Mr. Reddy. Mr. Reddy was born in 1925, and she first met him when she was ten or eleven. He had been on a long and painful search for an incarnation of the Divine Mother and finally found her in his own, young relative. He became her devotee, her spiritual father and protector.

Just like The Mother, Mother Meera spent a lot of time traveling outside of her physical body when she was young. Mr. Reddy recognized that this was most likely a yogic preparation for her future mission.

For a couple of years, he took her to different ashrams. One of them was the Sri Aurobindo Ashram in Pondicherry, where she would meet long-time devotees of Sri Aurobindo and The Mother. She never met the two sages while they were still alive, yet even as a child she often had visions of them both. The devotees were surprised that she had such spiritual knowledge without having been formally trained.

As a teenager, Mother Meera went to their ashram school. Then, in the late 1970s, she started to offer meditations and darshans in the Aurobindo ashram, though she never considered herself as their successor.

Mother Meera has always been able to transmit the supramental light. She says that she has never been on earth before this lifetime, and that before coming here, she knew who she was, that she would incarnate on earth, and what her work would be. She says that to give darshan as much as possible is her only interest. This is not to say that she is not involved in daily life as well. She has a small build but does not shy away from taxing physical labor; she's always working, carrying heavy loads, hammering away, mixing cement. She does come from very strong peasant stock. Even today, when there are construction demands, she does not seem to mind digging holes in the Indian soil in ninety-degree heat!

She has said that, during darshan, she is able to loosen some of the invisible spiritual knots of the people who sit with her by bringing through the supramental light. Sometimes she uses the terms "Paramatman Light" or simply the "Light." This divine light, which is of the Highest Self, activates each person's own inner light and illuminates all levels of their being. She can see whether a person who comes to her has already received darshan from her. Apparently, once the Light has descended, it is always there, whether people are aware of it or not. Spiritual progress does not depend on the number of darshans they attend but on people's devotion, dedication and sincerity.

Having gone to see Mother Meera for over 25 years now, I can testify, as most people do, that the experience is always different. It is also — each time — a mirroring of my own inner journey, of what is happening for me at that time.

The first time I saw her, I was working through my own mother issues. I dove deeply into my love and my connection with my mother, and at the same time became painfully aware of my anxiety and fear of suffocation and limitation. During those first four days I felt embraced by the archetype of the divine mother: a mother who has no expectations or limitations and is energetically able to offer the right kind of help.

During another visit, I was struggling to let go of a former teacher of mine who was more intent on using me than encouraging or empowering me to find myself. At that point, it was refreshing to receive the unwavering and unconditional support through Mother Meera. Absolutely delicious to feel that. It was a major turning point for me, a step forward in my warriorship. No longer would I give my personal power away to somebody else.

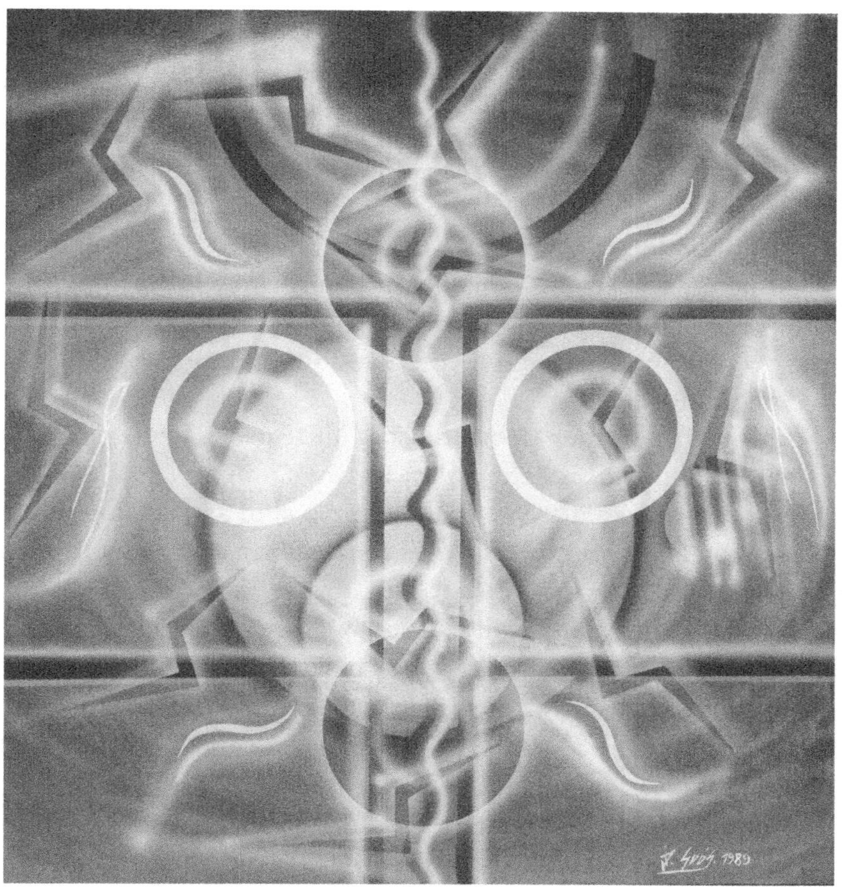

Later my darshans with her became much more impersonal. I would go into the formless, into the light, into the sound beyond the sound.

I love that the darshans of Mother Meera take place in deep, sacred silence beyond the dimension of words. Sometimes she gives as many as four darshan sessions a day, each time to about 200 people or more. Lately, after everybody has received their personal blessing from her, she remains seated and gives a blessing to the whole group for five to ten minutes. This collective blessing is so very powerful. She no longer touches people, and now keeps her eyes closed. She has said that she can still see all the people there. Sitting there in the room, I somehow know and feel that she does!

Until I met Mother Meera, most of my teachers were male, and most of them had a deep respect for the feminine. Still, Mother Meera provoked a distinct healing in me, and a balancing of the masculine and feminine. She has always attracted many men to her sessions, both in the U.S. and Europe. But when I first met her in Germany I was really struck by it; I saw so many elderly German men kneeling in front of her to receive her blessing. Each time she touched such a grey or bald head, I could sense in my own body and soul that part of the heavy German World War karma was being taken care of.

Mother Meera ended up in Germany because her uncle, Mr. Reddy, needed dialysis treatment. But was it by accident that they lived close to Hadamar? The Nazis did some of their most gruesome experiments in the Hadamar Euthanasia Center. Vivisections were performed on the brains of psychiatric patients. Many thousands of people with physical or mental disabilities, including numerous children, were either killed or sterilized. Is it part of the divine plan to send an avatar where vast healing is needed?

Mark Matousek has published a great memoir on his own journey with Mother Meera. He gave it a beautiful title: *Mother of the Unseen World: the Mystery of Mother Meera.* His connection with her started in 1984 when he first visited her, together with his travel companion, the celebrated mystic and author Andrew Harvey. He knew immediately, without knowing how he knew, that this person was unlike anyone he had ever seen before. He wrote that it was "*... as if she belonged to another species.*" Once he spent three long months in the dead of winter living in Mother Meera's house.

He also volunteered in the Mother Meera English Medium High School in South India, where she pays a monthly visit.

As time went on, he wished to ask her some questions for his book, in privacy. Somehow, the opportunity would never materialize, even though Mother Meera must have been well aware of his wish. She rarely gives formal interviews. But finally, when he had given up all hope, she did make time for him.

At one point, they were talking about the state of the world and the challenges facing human beings. I quote here the end of the interview...

Matousek: *There's so much danger and fear. When it comes to injustice, when is it right to fight back? To use anger? To take action in the service of the good?*

Mother Meera: *When your heart is clear, you may act. Otherwise, you only make things worse.*

Matousek: *Isn't it better to do something than nothing at all? Even if your heart's not completely clear?*

Mother Meera: *The destruction of the world is a human idea. Not a divine one.*

Matousek: *Many people are terrified. They think the world is about to end.*

Mother Meera: *Humanity will not be destroyed. There is nothing to fear.*

It is hard to fathom who Mother Meera really is and how she perceives "reality." This is probably true of all spiritual beings who have come to earth with a mission for humanity at large. It is possible to get a little glimpse of Mother Meera's world by looking at her paintings — a few can be seen on the Internet. They were published in 1989 in the book *Bringing Down the Light* (with an introduction by Andrew Harvey).

These mysterious paintings are watercolors by Mother Meera of the after-death states of her uncle, Mr. Reddy. They record her direct perception of the subtle realms through which he was traveling. They often show him being cared for by several divine mothers as he is sitting in a peaceful cave. In one of the paintings, Sri Aurobindo tells The Mother, "Our baby is coming" as the three are traveling in a boat. In another one, Mr. Reddy sits down to meditate, but is disturbed by many thoughts. In the next painting, made the day after, the thoughts have abated and a tree appears. I was touched by the sweet tenderness in all the paintings. And the light is everywhere....

- Whatsoever path they are following, they can come to me and I will help them to remember the Divine and give them peace and happiness when they are in trouble.
- The whole purpose of my work is in calling down the Paramatman Light and in helping people. For this I came—to open your hearts to the Light.
- Be like a child—clear, loving, spontaneous, infinitely flexible and ready each moment to wonder and accept a miracle.

The blessings of Divine Mother

Welcome your feelings, your thoughts, your bodily sensations
and then invite Divine Mother to touch your heart
with her magical fingers so it can fully open and soften
and sing its song of eternal love.

You may gently bow to her
as she is administering this healing to your heart.

An attitude of devotion
awakens the wonder of the innocent child in you.

This child is not jaded yet.
It is in touch with the unseen worlds.

It speaks to the animals, to the fairies and it is surrounded by playmates.

If you could allow this sense of wonder, of enthusiasm,
of adventure back into your life.

The blessings of Divine Mother are given to anyone who asks.

In her presence worries dissipate
and gratitude and generosity are generated from deep inside of you.

As the mother of the universe
she protects her children from harm and ignorance.

When you sit in her presence you realize how precious this life is, how precious you are and how incredible the plan for cosmic evolution is.

Divine Mother blesses you again and will remain available if you so choose.

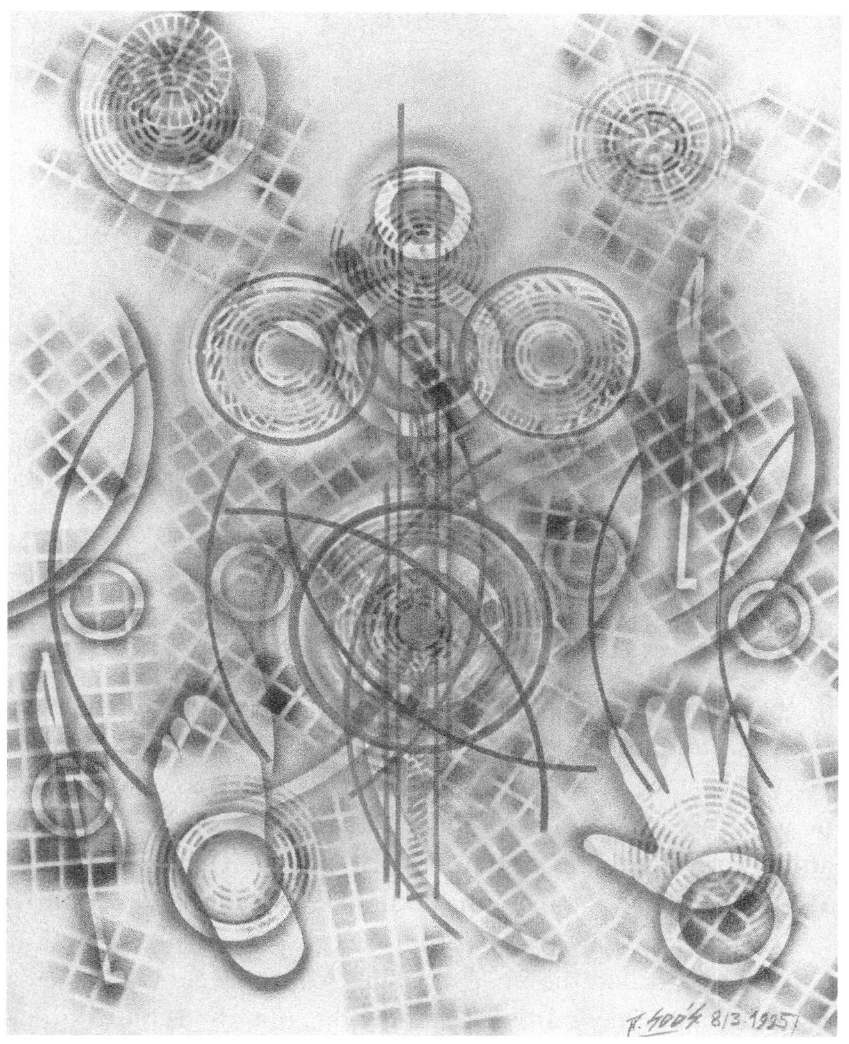

CHAPTER 12.

AMMA — the Hugging Saint

A MAJOR TEACHING OF this book is that the most potent way to change the world is through recognizing our true nature. Once we do, we understand deeply that we are not separate from each other or from the rest of the world. At the same time, many of the *Inspired Guidances* are also a call to action to end social injustice, and to protect and honor the planet while we still can.

Amma is the prime example of working energetically with people from a place of supreme divinity, while offering physical and financial help all over the world where it is most needed. Whenever there is a big natural disaster in the world, Amma is one of the first to be ready with resources.

Amma is called the hugging saint. No other person has ever demonstrated unconditional love by hugging thousands of people daily. She is sometimes at it for more than 20 hours, and it is not uncommon for Amma to go several days without sleep. If you like, you can watch this yourself in the fascinating documentary *Darshan,* in which Amma is giving a hug to 45,000 people in a non-stop 21-hour marathon festival! It has been estimated that by 2016 Amma had hugged 34 million people. And the great majority of people who receive a hug from her testify that they experienced something very special.

One day Kathy and I were in Germany for a series of darshans with Mother Meera. As we were about to take a local train to do some sightseeing, we saw a Russian devotee of hers boarding an earlier train in another direction. She was traveling back to her home in New York and struggling with some hefty suitcases. We helped her, and as her train was about to leave, she shouted to us, "*Do you have Amma's schedule for the next year?*" I said no, and she pulled a crumpled sheet of Amma's world tour out of her pocket and threw it to us as her train was already pulling out of the station.

I had wanted to see Amma for a long time, but somehow it had never materialized. I saw on the world tour sheet that she was coming to Belgium when I would be there and was able to adjust my own schedule accordingly.

Amma's transmission style is very different from Mother Meera's. For me though, it is clear that — in essence — they are undertaking a very similar planetary mission. They are undoing the nefarious effects of a very long spell of dominance by the patriarchal ideology, and restoring dignity, equality, accountability and compassion. Mother Meera and Amma are using the subtle energy of the heart, and miraculously, the times now are ready for it. Amma has given millions of people a heartfelt hug, often while whispering a mantra into their ears.

A year after I had been thrown her schedule (a gift from one divine mother to another one), I was sitting in front of Amma in Belgium. My brother Filip and his wife Christina were squatting there with me. She took the three of us in her arms, going back and forth from one to the other. In my mind's eye I saw a shimmering of multiple sacred geometric forms and her mantra was the sweetest of sounds, even though I could not remember later what I saw or heard. I found this visual, auditory and tactile transmission extraordinarily satisfying and nourishing. I was propelled into a vibrant, cosmic reality with which I knew, in an instant, my being is in constant contact, whether I am consciously aware of this or not. I was a bit embarrassed that Amma seemed to take an exceptionally long time with me. Later it turned out this had not been the case at all. During the hugging, time had simply stood still for me!

I love this passage from Rick Archer's (interviewer at Buddha at the Gas Pump website) introduction to a great book about Amma, written by Ram Das Batchelder.

> *I have interviewed quantum physicists who suggest that consciousness is not a product of brain functioning, but the source and essence of the manifest universe. They further suggest that since consciousness is the ultimate level from which creation is governed, all the laws of nature reside there. Mastery of the field of consciousness by someone like Amma can therefore open up possibilities most people would consider miraculous.*
>
> *Every time I receive Amma's embrace, I sense that she sits at the master switchboard of creation, sees deeply into my soul, and fine-tunes my life, providing subtle guidance which I can only dimly fathom, but which I'm certain has accelerated my spiritual progress profoundly. (Batchelder, Rising in Love: My Wild and Crazy Ride to Here and Now, with Amma, the Hugging Saint)*

Amma was born in 1953 to a family of fishermen in Kerala, southern India. Her formal name is Mata Amritanandamayi, which means "Divine Mother of Immortal Bliss." This has not always been her name. Her parents called her Sudhamani. By the time she was nine years old, her mother had given birth thirteen times. Amma was the fourth of eight surviving children.

From the various biographies written about Amma's childhood, a picture emerges of very hard circumstances. She was ridiculed and abused due to her unusual skin color. Unlike her parents, who were light skinned, Amma's skin had a dark blue hue which would change much later into dark brown. Amma was treated quite cruelly and had to become an obedient servant to the family and relatives — particularly her mother (who had become chronically ill after so many childbirths) and her older brother, who were both outright antagonistic towards her.

Besides her dark skin, she displayed strange, unchildlike behavior which did not sit well with her family. At the tender age of six months she already started to speak Malayalam, her mother tongue. By age two she was singing songs in praise of Krishna without having received formal instruction. At five she began composing devotional songs.

Amma herself has said,

> *From birth itself I had an intense liking for the Divine Name. I would repeat the Lord's Name incessantly with every breath, and a constant flow of divine thoughts was kept up in my mind irrespective of the place where I was or the work I was attending to. This unbroken recollection of God with love and devotion would be of immense help to any aspirant in attaining Divine Realization. (Swami Amritaswarupananda)*

She spent the little free time she had in meditation, longing for Krishna. The villagers considered her to be one who dwelt in another world. In addition to her many household chores, she would take food and clothing from her house and distribute them to the poor. Her father became very concerned about her for fear that she had gone insane. He ended up locking her outside of the family house.

One day, at age 21, Amma overheard people singing devotional songs to Krishna. Divine bliss descended on her and her appearance transformed spontaneously into the movements and features of Krishna. Even her skin took on the blue hue of

Krishna. This event marked her first manifestation of "the divine mood of Krishna," or *Krishna Bhava*. Amma began manifesting *Devi Bhava*, "the mood of the Divine Mother," about six months after the advent of *Krishna Bhava*. Her mission had started to acquire its own form and definition. *Devi* is a name of the Divine Mother and *Krishna* of course refers to the most well-known (and most joyful!) of Indian avatars.

A format developed in which Amma would begin with the *Krishna Bhava* program in the early evening, hugging her devotees until midnight. In this state Amma reveals her oneness and identity with Krishna. After a short break, she would continue till the early morning hours with the *Devi Bhava* part of the program, in which all devotees who want will receive Devi's embrace. In this state Amma reveals her oneness and identity with the Divine Mother.

I am reminded of that other Indian saint and mystic in the bhakti tradition, Sri Ramakrishna (1836-1886). He proclaimed the oneness of all religions and intensely worshipped the blissfulness of the Divine Mother. He would talk to his disciples about the development of *bhava* as a very intense state of mystical union. (Hixon, *Great Swan: Meetings with Ramakrishna*)

Many villagers around Amma initially assumed that Amma was being possessed by various deities. Amma herself would see it somewhat differently. In this quote she talks about herself in the third person (as she often does) and explains a bit more about *Devi Bhava:*

> *All the deities represent the infinite aspects of the One Supreme Being, which exists within us as well. A divine personality can manifest any one of them by his or her mere will for the good of the world. Devi Bhava is the manifestation of the Eternal Feminine, the active principle of the Impersonal Absolute.*

It should be remembered that all objects having a name or form are mere mental projections. Why should a doctor wear a white coat, or a policeman a uniform and cap? All these are merely external aids meant to create a certain impression. In a like manner, Amma dons the garb of Devi in order to give strength to the devotional attitude of the people. The Universal Spirit that is in me is also within you. If you can realize that Indivisible Principle that is ever shining in you, you will become one with That. (Dayalu, Amma: Inspiring Experiences with the Divine Mother)

More from Amma about *Devi Bhava*:

If you were to really see Amma as she is, it would overwhelm you — you couldn't possibly bear it. Because of this, Amma always covers herself with a thick layer of maya, illusion. But during Devi Bhava, Mother removes one or two of her veils, revealing a little more of what she really is. (Batchelder, Rising in Love)

The scope of worldly projects that Amma is involved with is mind boggling — simply staggering!

At present (2018), Amma has consecrated more than twenty "Brahmasthanam" temples. These temples are quite unique and are open to anyone for worship, irrespective of their religion. The central icon is four-sided — Ganesha, Shiva, Devi and the Serpent — emphasizing the inherent unity that underlies the manifold aspects of the divine.

The Amma University, Amrita Vishwa Vidyapeetham, offers over 200 undergraduate, postgraduate and doctoral programs. It collaborates with top universities in the U.S. and Europe. It has been in existence for 15 years and has been ranked as the 8th best university in India by the Indian government. Its medical school offers a dual-degree program in business with the State University of New York at Buffalo.

Part of the Amma University is the Amrita Institute of Medical Science and Research (AIMS), which has received several National Healthcare Excellence Awards. Many patients are treated for free.

Amma is a huge fund-raiser everywhere in the world, and especially in India, where people have more trust in her than they do in the government. She has assumed responsibility for orphanages, regular and special needs schools with free education for poor children, hospices for the terminally ill, housing and shelter for the homeless, pension programs for destitute women, and free food distribution. She also offers this in the United States through "Mother's Kitchen."

Amma's superhuman characteristics enable her to hug millions of people and — at the same time — organize vast humanitarian aid efforts. No wonder Pulitzer Prize Winner Alice Walker calls her the most heroic person she has probably ever met, and says that Amma presents the kind of leadership we need for our planet to survive. Jane Goodall has said about her, "*She is God's love in a human body*."

There are many speeches and comments available by Amma. Here are some that you may enjoy reading:

- Human beings are not the only ones with the capacity for speech. Animals, birds and plants have this power, but we do not have the capacity to understand. One who has the Vision of the Self knows all these things.
- It is often said that factories pollute the air, but there is even a greater poison within the human being, and that is the ego.

- Everyone in the world should be able to sleep without fear, at least for one night. Everyone should be able to eat to his or her fill, at least for one day. There should be at least one day when hospitals see no one admitted due to violence. By doing selfless service for at least one day, everyone should help the poor and needy. It is Amma's prayer that at least this small dream be realized.
- When the disciple approaches the Master, he is raw, rusty, primitive. The Master, the infinitely loving, divine alchemist, transforms the disciple into pure gold.
- The mind is nothing but thoughts. Thoughts, when intense, become actions. Actions, when repeated, become habits. Habits form character. Therefore, to get rid of the mind, first we should change the quality of our thoughts.
- Death is not complete annihilation. It is a pause. It is like pressing the pause button on a tape recorder in the middle of a song. Sooner or later, when pressed again, the pause button is released and the song continues.
- My religion is Love.

Divine Mother in her many forms

In meditation you are not afraid to be with what is.

The sacred reality of what is, is always right here.

It is a reality beyond fear.

No effort is needed to experience this.
Just openness.

Just remembering what you really are is enough.

Remembering is surrendering.

You are as much pure love now as you will ever be.
Again — you are as much pure love now as you will ever be.

This insight liberates you.

It is the direct path.

No more pain from thinking that you would be separated from a goal in a faraway future.

Your dedicated presence consists
in refusing to identify with what you are not.

In this way you are shifting from a fear-based self to an ever-loving self.

Mighty planetary forces are supporting your practice.

Divine Mother in her many forms — Sweet Mother, Mother Meera, Amma, Anandamayi Ma, Sarada Devi, Kwan Yin, Avalokiteshvara — blesses your inner being over and over.

In the middle of outside chaos your one-pointed concentration is on that which never changes — your true self.

No postponing.
You are as much pure love now as you will ever be.

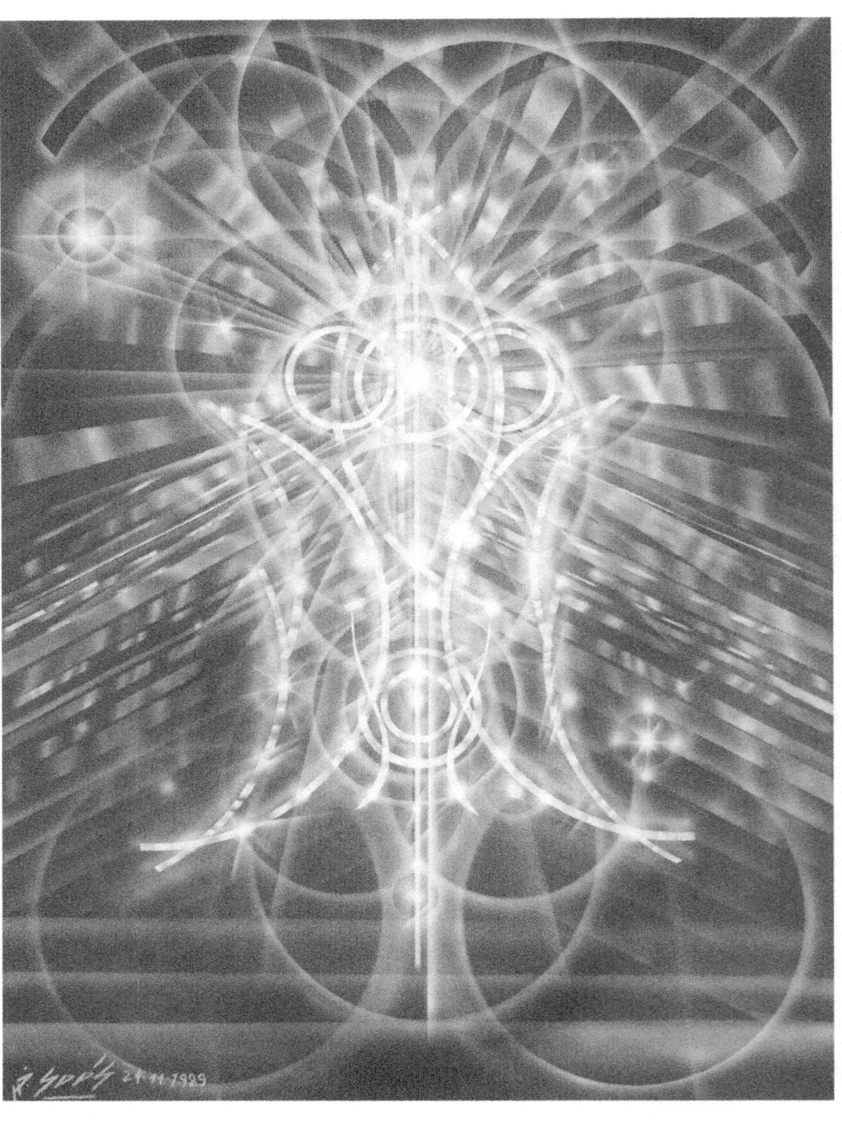

Part 4. Inspired Guidances

I TOLD YOU IN Part 1 about the synchronistic series of circumstances that led me to solemnly promise to do my best to receive *words of wisdom*. I gave my word to do so during a remarkable session with a medium in London in 1991. Now, more than 25 years later, the *Inspired Guidances* (as I decided to name them) still keep coming.

I said *yes* because that is what I truly wanted. My rational mind did not understand what I was agreeing to, but by then I had already freed myself from the severe limitations of that part of my mind. My heart definitely wanted to serve a dimension or reality of a higher order — if it possibly existed —and to serve it well. I had been studying, after all, under a whole series of masters, each one a spiritual warrior in their own right, who had said yes to their task. In comparison, what was asked of me looked minimal. That being said, I agonized and even trembled about how to materialize my promise.

It is still astonishing to me that my promise has come to fruition. Whenever I sit down to open myself to receive some words of wisdom, almost always in the presence of other people who are meditating with me in silence, some sentences do come. It never fails. I experience it as a mixture of mediumship and conscious channeling. Often the words that arise take the form of guided meditations. Sometimes they will refer specifically to current world events. If they are delivered in the context of a workshop I am teaching, they also address the process the participants are in.

As the words arise, there is a quite beautiful gathering of presence or consciousness for me. And always an opening of the heart chakra. In my body, I feel a vibrational shift. Looking back, I can see how so much of my life has prepared me for this.

Now I know for sure that it all started with my near-death experience at the age of four; I realize that it must have opened me, as an initiation. My work with my Hungarian shamanic teacher was another big step. Also, my intense quest for the nature of true reality, supported by the discipline of 45 years of daily meditation, has enabled me to tap into dimensions of the sacred — and their very uplifting and intense levels of a "higher" frequency.

CHAPTER 1

Guides and Angels of Light, Love and Peace

WHO OR WHAT ARE the guides of light, love and peace that so often address us in the following collection of meditations? Do they arise from my (or our) collective imagination, or do they live some sort of independent existence? And in which dimension would this be? Would it be helpful to put them in the same category as angels? But does this even make any sense in today's world, dominated as it is by science and the rational mind?

How can we grasp the consciousness of plants, of stars and galaxies? Is there a new breed of angel available in an ever-evolving universe? Is it possible — with the help of guides and angels — to make the world into a sacred place?

Probably such questions will always fascinate me, and probably you as well, dear reader. I doubt that I will ever come to firm conclusions. It is true, though, that the nature of my work brings me in almost daily contact with experiences that *do* point to other dimensions of reality.

To give just four examples:

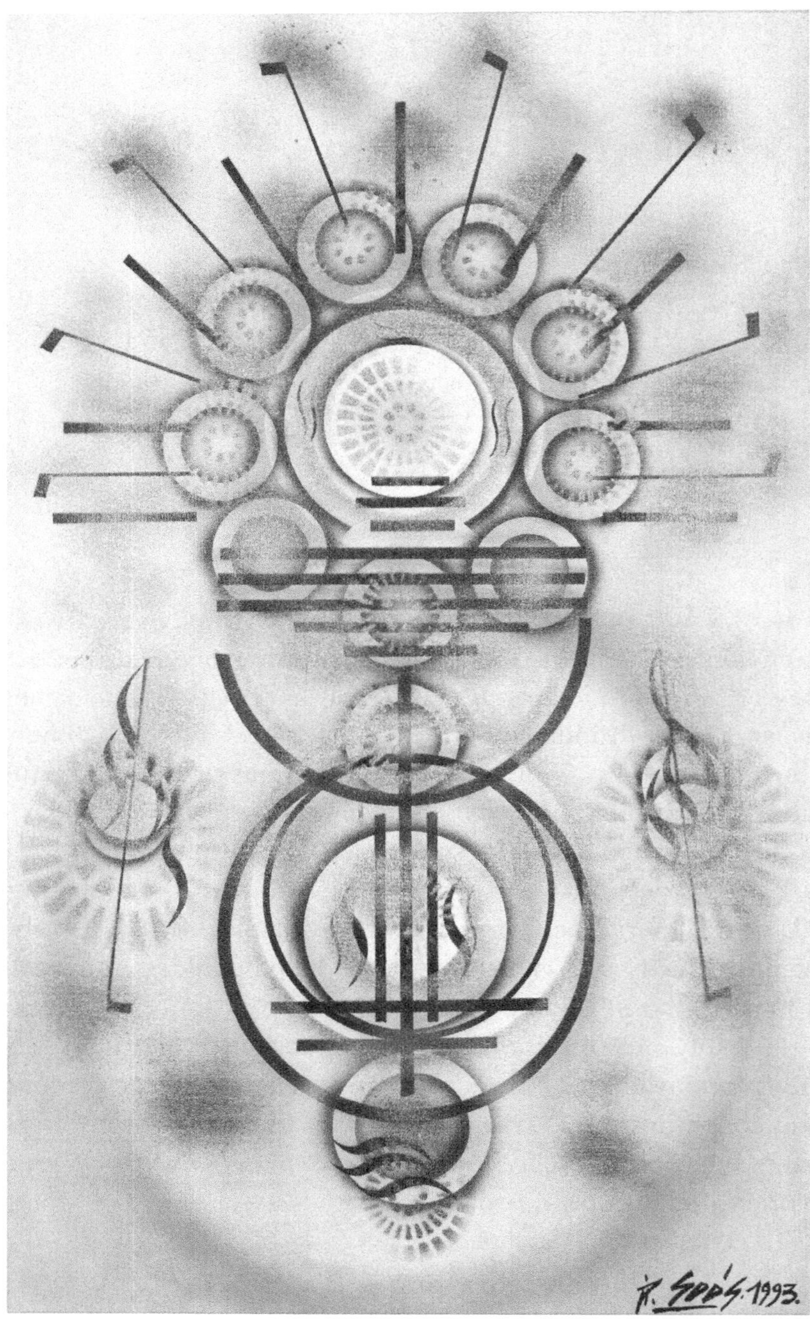
R. Söös. 1993.

- When I perform a Reiki initiation, Dr. Mikao Usui is often distinctly present. Colleagues and students feel this as well. For me, his presence manifests as a palpable strength in my legs, a warmth around my heart, and a clarity and preciseness of purpose.
- A boy of twelve that I initiated has a special, lucid dream about Usui — even before the Reiki class started.
- When I gave Reiki to a Taekwondo master in a hospital and told him that I felt the presence of his grandfather, he lost control. As this guarded and very disciplined man broke down sobbing, he confided that as a boy he experienced love only from his grandfather.
- Some of my shamanic students can describe in detail and with great clarity my teacher Jóska Soós, whom they have never met. They might hear him say something, or they use an expression that I can immediately identify as "Jóska." Some even see his teacher Tamas, whom I have never met and of whom we have no pictures.

I could easily fill page after page with similar examples.

Instead, I will cite here just one interesting observation from the renowned saint Sri Ramakrishna. He told his devotees that during one phase of his spiritual development, when he sat down for meditation, a young man who looked very much like him would emerge from his own body and seat himself in front of him and guide him. (Arun Shourie)

In the early years of the *Inspired Guidance* coming through, while I was wondering a lot about the existence of ascended masters and angels, I found an astonishing testimony. It is one of the most moving and authentic documents I have come across. The whole story is recorded in a book by Gitta Mallasz (1907-1992), a long-time international bestseller called *Talking with Angels*. Everyone who reads it is touched by it. The remarkable events in the book took place in a small village during the Second World War in Hungary.

Gitta and her three Jewish friends, Hanna, Josef, and his wife Lili, were getting together every week during the terrible period of the occupation by the Nazis. They were acutely aware that even more frightening times were on their way. Then they made a firm decision — they wanted to support each other on their inner path, no matter what happened.

One afternoon in June 1943, Hanna suddenly cried out, "Pay attention, it is not me who is talking." Her voice sounded different, and during the next 17 months she spoke aloud very specific messages for each of the four friends. The last conversation ended with the words, "Believe: the Eternal Life is already yours."

Gitta wrote everything down. The instructions for them were clearly coming from a world filled with love and an amazing intelligence. Among themselves, the foursome called the spiritual beings who were addressing them their "angels." Gitta, the only non-Jewish one, would be the only one to survive this gruesome war period.

The evening before the deportation of Josef — to what turned out to be the concentration camp where he would die — one of the angels mentioned that the four of them could only act effectively if they worked together. The angels saw them as the voices of the *New Song*. It was not important whether they would be together physically. This *New Song*, the angels said, is the new frequency, "*...tuned into the Divine — it is called Light.*"

In 1976, after more than 30 years, Gitta finally made public the notes she took during those 17 months. I think that this shows divine wisdom as well, because at that time, a larger readership — for whom all this was intended — was ready and open enough to understand and absorb those messages.

The divine plan in action! My friend Ian Graham, with whom I travelled to Bhutan, expressed this idea very well in the title of his book *God is Never Late...But Never Early Either.*

I like the sound of the phrase, the *New Song*. You will see that I have put a selection of the meditations I have been receiving concerning the "new times" in Part 4, Chapter 3: "The New Age and a Call for Action."

I personally feel a great kinship with the messages and the vibrational quality of the angels, as documented by Gitta. A similar quality is present in the tone of the *Inspired Guidances*. The voice that speaks to us wants to connect with the listener or the reader. It certainly connects by inspiring and guiding, but also by activating innate knowledge. At other times, the words that come are healing and protecting.

For those of you who are interested in more speculation and information about angels, I also recommend a dialogue that took place between the Christian theologian Matthew Fox and the scientist Rupert Sheldrake. The gist of it is to be found in their book *The Physics of Angels: Exploring the Realm where Science and Spirit Meet*.

They say that other forms of consciousness— besides the human form — almost certainly exist in the cosmos. Probably angels have been in existence since the beginning of the universe and can be considered to be those who concern themselves with the regulating of nature.

Sheldrake points out how, following Einstein, we can now see how mutual interconnectivity is mediated through gravitational fields, all contained within the gravitational field of the universe, the "universal field."

Maybe angels played a role to help in the awakening of human imagination and intuition. In this way, they have a special bond with prophets, artists and shamans.

Allow now the "Guides and Angels of Light, Love and Peace" to address themselves very specifically to you. When the words and sentences of the meditations are coming through, I often feel myself in contact with the heavenly dimensions. Maybe this will happen for you as well....

The angel of peace and healing

What are you?
Where do you come from?
Where are you going?

During your meditation these existential questions are being answered.

Somehow, inexplicably and mysteriously,
you are shifting in consciousness and you become the knowing.

This knowing is not dry and has nothing to do with the intellect.
This knowing arises out of loving and being.

It is the understanding that there is no birth and there is no death.

It is the understanding that there is only a continuation of consciousness.

May the angel of peace and healing reveal this truth to you, now.

A sense of deep peace, profound peace and relaxation
comes over you as you are living in this truth.

You experience that your loved ones are not gone.
They are living in your heart forever.

On occasion they come to pay you a visit from the subtle dimensions.

Be open to experience this, knowing that love transcends time and space.

Shamans have always traveled through the dimensions
searching to decipher the mysteries of the universe.

You must be ready for this journey.
Your mind activity has become quiet.

Your heart has been expanding.
Your being is ready for its next adventure.

Can you see them or feel them?
All the avatars are here: all the bodhisattvas, the teachers, the guides, the angels.

Sitting in the eternity of consciousness purifies all karma,
abolishes fear and establishes you in the peace beyond all understanding.

With the eyes of the Christ, of the Buddha, of Krishna

Your sacred Self always abides in the Christ, in the Buddha,
in Krishna, in the Light of Creation, in the Splendor of the Formless.

Remembering this, knowing this, celebrating this,
you can connect with your essence

in the blink of an eye,
right now.

It does not matter much which concepts you believe in.
It matters tremendously that you know what you are.

Why would Creation withhold Perfection from you,
at any moment?

Can you turn inside
and look with the eyes of the Christ, of the Buddha, of Krishna?

Looking like this is true seeing
and transforms illusions into the one Reality.

There is no need to look back now.
You have reached your destiny.
You live and embody the Reality beyond any divisions.
You are free.

Be what you are.
Love what you are.
All is well.

Sophia

Make space in your heart for Sophia, the goddess of wisdom.
She wants to teach you today.

Trust that which can never leave you — your real Self.

As it becomes the relaxed focus of your open attention
it pulls you beyond the mental concepts
into the heart of all that is.

No excessive effort.
Just stay here and receive refreshing rest.

It is simple and easy to live here
and to let yourself be loved here.

Fully present in this moment
you taste eternity in its ever-unfolding magic.

Magic is always right where you are.
When you take the time to be.

Magic and miracles and mystery and love
are the ingredients of your ongoing self-realization.

Your real self is already perfectly and completely realized.
Knowing this stabilizes your happiness.

Know thyself.
Know thyself as peace and everlasting love.

The message of the masters

Listen now to the message from the masters.
It is beautiful and simple.

Do not despair about how to reach your spiritual destiny.
It resides in your willingness to reside in the perfection of
this moment.

This includes your openness to see yourself as completely lovable
as you are right now.

You do not have to pay any dues to be willing to see yourself like this.

This is what happens.
The recognition of your own lovability, which is a fact,
reveals the brilliance of everything around you.

You can rest peacefully now in knowing that this is so.

Just be ready to receive the gift.
Each moment is a pearl of perfection.

Ongoing surrendering to the totality
of what this moment has to offer
is the master key.

In this way your life flows naturally and spontaneously.
Love is your source
and is always pulling you to itself.

Guides (1)

Your guides are very happy to be here for you.

As the transmission is about to begin
check and see if you are sufficiently supported
by the earth right now.
Can you allow an even deeper sense of nourishment?
Take your time for this.

Now establish yourself in the middle of a huge pillar of light,
starting from beneath your feet and legs
and rising very high into the sky.

Magnificent angels of various manifestations
are going up and down this column of light.
Sometimes they are brushing very close to you
and when they do you feel sparkles of delight
exploding in the cells of your being.

Take a moment to orient yourself towards your basic chakras
and investigate if they are fully present and open.
The root chakra, sexual center, solar plexus, your heart center,
the throat, the third eye center, the crown
and many more chakras, as yet somewhat unknown and inviting you
to be more active in your consciousness right now.

All these chakras are being activated through a network of love.

The more embodied you are in the earth
the more you can extend above her and beyond her.

You are a part now of whole galaxies of light coming into being.

So much light, so much love.
The journey inside is astounding.

Guides (2)

As always, your guides, your protectors, your teachers
are here and they are supporting you.
Let them get close so they can help even more.

If you notice anything that is worrying you, that is oppressing you,
gently put it to the side
and let it dissolve into the big openness of your original nature.

You are not suppressing anything.
You are just paying attention to what is also there for you, right now.

Centered in your heart,
you are stretched out in all the directions.

Each of the directions is blessing you with its strength,
its support, its wisdom and its love.

All of the directions are living in you.
Let them gift you now with their beautiful essence.

The West, the North, the East, the South, the Above and the Below
are holding you so you can occupy the vastness safely and consciously.

The vast space welcomes you as you are.

You are discovering that your original nature has no real limitations.

Your body is cosmic.
That which is witnessing this
is beyond time and space altogether.

Guides (3)

The guides and teachers who are near and dear to you
are greeting you and are offering you all their support.

Real life reveals itself
when you no longer identify with the excessive activities of the mind.

Position yourself beyond the mind
in the field of love and forgiveness and beauty
which touches you so deeply that it transforms you
into what you really are.

Any time you spend in this realm is highly beneficial.
There is no worrying here.
There is deep accepting and embracing of the mystery that you are.

The world (1)

As the world grows noisier
you are being asked, quite directly,
to become a keeper of the holy silence.

Blessed by your inner silence
even the burden of the many activities
is being taken away.

Yogis from the past, Sri Aurobindo and Sweet Mother,
Babaji and Yogananda, and many others,
and yogis from the present and the future times
are helping you to contact the depth of that silence.

This silence is super alive.
It is knowing and not knowing.
It is love and understanding, truth and beauty.

Sharing presence is the great gift of being in silence.

Jesus, Buddha, Mahavir, Krishna.
Because of their silence their words are still so very potent.

The world (2)

In a noisy world, one glimpse of inner silence
sets into motion a transformation
from what is superficial to what is essential.

The guides and teachers, and there are many,
support you in recognizing the beauty of your essence.

Can you see that your essence is not of this world?
That it is eternal, beyond death, beyond all fear?

Your essence is generous and gratitude is its nature.

Have no fear.
Your essence is indestructible.

The avatars

Invite the avatars to join you
as you are gently surrendering into meditating.

The company you keep reflects
what it is you want from existence —
love, support and empowerment
to live according to your highest potential.

Use your intention and your imagination
to propel yourself into, and as, boundless space.
See if you can maintain this for a while.

You are not escaping from the world or from yourself.
Far from it.
You are occupying the space
that matches your awake presence.

.... Remember the avatars are still joining you...

Mental activity becomes so insignificant
as you have morphed into the vast, open space.

Your heart, on the other hand,
finally finds the freedom to express herself
as the manifestation of the caring mother of the whole universe.

Your mystic nature embraces heaven and earth
and is not fooled by seeming separation.

A jump in evolution is not unrealistic

Listen.
Listen to the softness of the rain and relax into it
as sweetly, as deeply, as completely as you possibly can.

Your true nature has no need for refinement.
It is absolutely perfect as it is.

You cannot even remember its birth
since it has never been subjected
to the human-made laws of time.

But the masters, any master of truth and wisdom,
do encourage you to remember what you really are.

One glimpse.
Even one single glimpse of this
will reveal more than any Scripture can.

It takes you to the deep stillness
out of which all activity and all non-activity arise.

It takes you to the all-pervading love
beyond the distractions of the mind.

Many have come before you, your spiritual ancestors,
who have walked the earth knowing what they are.
Now there are so many of you,
a jump in evolution is not unrealistic.

May everlasting peace descend upon you as you remember
constantly, vigilantly and very lovingly
what you are and always will be.

Shalom!
Peace!
Ananda!

Your sanctuary is the ever-present quiet inside of you

Your sanctuary is the ever-present quiet inside of you.

When fear and emotionality and divisiveness
are running through the collective,
the lovers of peace are naturally holding space for everyone.

Your heart has been designed to do just that.
Through love and compassion
it takes down the walls of separation.

You came into manifest form
to celebrate the unity, the uniqueness and the diversity of all beings.

From the wellspring of your deepening quiet
intelligent action may arise
on occasion and only when needed.

In awakened consciousness you are like the bodhisattva.
You are aware of the needs of the world
and you help as you can.

May all be blessed by the sincerity of your aspiration.

You are being used as a channel for goodness

Invite yourself into the beautiful state of vigilance and alertness
and simultaneously allow for the feelings of tenderness and gentleness.
Explore this interesting combination —
vigilance/alertness, gentleness/tenderness.

Follow the movement of your breath
and let it lead you to a place of centeredness.

Notice how strong your foundation has become now
and how your energy field is extending very wide in all directions.

From this place of wide extension, visualize, as best you can,
all your chakras lined up as a huge column of light.

Sitting solidly in all this brilliance
allow some of the suffering and destruction in the world
to penetrate your heart and let the transformation begin.

In this process your heart is becoming bigger, even shinier.
The transmutation makes the chakras, all the chakras, light up even more.

Magnificent beings of light and love
are pouring their energies through as well.

Because of the purity of your intentions
you can trust that you are being used as a channel for goodness.

Rumi

Please feel yourself very welcome here.
Just be at ease with yourself.
You really are good as you are.

True meditating is a supreme form of intimacy.

There is no pressure on you, no expectations.

You are willing to be open and available and that is more than enough.

Intimacy with yourself and your surroundings is really what you want.

You are not being judged; you are being loved.

Intimacy is exploring what takes place when your heart is more tender.

You start to remember the openness you have always been.

You are so present, you are not even waiting for something to happen.

Every so often thoughts disappear.
This does not bother you or frighten you.

You have entered the realm beyond the ego, beyond the known.
The realm of being.
Explore and enjoy.

This realm is empty and unformed
and at the same time buzzing with potential and creativity.
It is very activating to be here.

Here it is easy to be grateful for this moment, for this day, for this life.

Rumi, the great mystic, says, be with those who help you be.

The last step is not taken by you

A few precious moments every day
dedicated to fully remembering what you are and always will be.

Also, every day, a few golden moments
to call upon the inspiration of your beloved guides and teachers.

When you receive a glimpse of your true nature
you discover that the journey is not endless.
What you are, appears right in front of you.

It is always there, so incredibly close.

You cannot grasp it.
You can give it space.
You can give it your heart as an entryway.

You have to want it really badly.
You also have to be really relaxed and cool about it.

You have to trust the moments of revelation.
The light that is there.

The love.
The knowing.

Fear not.
Your time has come.
The door stands open, wide open.

The last step is not taken by you.
Grace does it for you.

You are so loved, beyond your comprehension,
for what you are.

The spirits

The spirits of the trees, the spirits of the mountains,
the benevolent spirits of the earth all around you
are witnessing and supporting your meditation.

Just as you have a great chance now to witness
the depth and the beauty of your being.
It is such a marvel!

Witnessing is not being removed or aloof.
It is watching with wonder how the sacred
always wants to be more intimate with you.

Modern life has much to offer
and yet you yearn for more connection
with what matters most to you —
feeling love, being love, sharing love.

Your dear friends, the animal spirits, the plant spirits,
the crystal spirits are supporting you.
In meditation their consciousness and your consciousness
are touching each other and lifting each other up.

They also teach you to be in the very beneficial state of
no-mind.

No-mind intensifies silence, natural presence,
aliveness, peacefulness, expectancy.

Your dear friends are always watching you with compassion,
wondering how they can help you the most
in matters of love and the celebration of all life.

All the time, all the time
you are being held by the love you are.

Ask the angels to help

Please come home — to what you really are.
You want to be free from everything that could possibly
diminish you.

Ask the angels to help.
You ask. They come.
It is as simple as that.

Right now, as you are sitting so quietly
there is a freeing of contractions in your body,
in your emotions and in your psyche.

Let it happen, just like this.

There is no hurry in this process of surrendering to your innate freedom.
It is ongoing.

Angels are doing their work
while you are giving up resistance.

Everything is possible.
It is happening for many beings.
Why not for you?

Now your being is communing with the beingness of the entire universe.

Transmission at the level of being is sacred.
It establishes everything in its original freedom.

Select one person

Select one person
to whom you would like to dedicate your meditation.
Connect from heart to heart,
from your high Self to their high Self.
On the bridge between the two of you
angels of light and love are going back and forth.
Let happiness fill every fiber of your being!

Happiness *is* your true nature.
You can feel it easily when you give yourself away
to serve, to heal, to share.

In meditation you leave the person
and the problems far behind you
and you dip into divine consciousness
which shines abundantly for everyone,
everywhere, all the time.

When you receive this light
you can see your perfection.
You remember your original face.
Your journey has brought you back once again.
As many times as you get lost,
come back to the perfection of this moment.

Meditation is the art
to profoundly celebrate this moment
and only this moment.
How simple!
How beautiful!

Divine Mother

Receive the frequency of pure love.

Receive it first in the heart, with warmth and with strength,
and then let it spread on a cellular level throughout the body.

Imagine that many angels, under the guidance of Divine Mother,
are facilitating this process for you.

Dedicate your transformation to the coming into being
of a more beautiful world.

A world where peace and harmony and justice walk hand in hand.

New manifestation always arises first from the inner planes of consciousness.

When you tune in to the frequency of pure love
the veil of ignorance lifts away.

Beyond the veil you experience your true self.
Your true self, which never dies, is pure love.

Meher Baba

Every breath you take
is divine presence breathing through you.

When you have become quiet enough to notice this presence
you have stepped through the veil.

In the light you can see that you have been created
for loving, for receiving and for giving back.

The great mystic Meher Baba observed,
being is dying by loving.

For quite a while, humanity has been standing here at this threshold.
Only through love can it make the quantum leap.

Every individual contribution has cosmic significance.
That is the meaning of your life on earth.

When you choose for love, you have already won.
What love creates, can never be undone.

The root system of the big forest trees

First of all, become one with the root system of the big forest trees
and let them pull you down, down, down into the earth
and give you a very strong and stable foundation.

These giant elders love you.
Feel it in your heart.

As you keep sinking deeper and deeper into the ground
start extending your physical body into the four directions
all around you.

More and more space becomes available.
Raise now your energy field high into the heavens,
like Jacob's ladder,
and be available to commune with the cosmic masters.

They are present for you, always.
Their wisdom is yours.
You could see them as extensions of yourself.

Guest of Honor

Once again this would be the perfect time
to welcome the Guest of Honor into your tender heart space.

Even if you are a bit shy about this invitation
surrender to it anyway.

There is nothing like being in the arms of the true Beloved.

You have been invited many times before.
Would you agree that you are more ready than ever?

The Sacred Guest knows that this is your deepest longing
and that nothing but this will satisfy you.

Avalokiteshvara

The great Avalokiteshvara shares her heart energy with you.
As she reaches inside of you
she removes the old
and activates the new.

Allow the softening to take place,
passing through the veil of the mental
and establishing yourself in the miracle of the natural.

To be open like this is your natural state.
The primordial energy has received you back in her womb.

Here your deepest needs are met.
You are no longer under the laws of time and space.
You are rediscovering your original face.

These are eternal moments of grace.
Avalokiteshvara is still holding your heart.
From now on you will never be apart.

Angels of mercy

Can the heart absorb the tremendous pain of the world?
Yes, it can.

In your courage to feel sorrow
there is such an aliveness connecting you
with all of humanity.

As you breathe in
are you willing to be with all beings who are suffering?

As you breathe out
your mind and heart are one
and know how to heal any situation.

Breathing in suffering, breathing out love.

Breathing in shame, breathing out your natural goodness.
It is much bigger than you can know.

The angels of mercy are with you now.
All around you and in you.

Deep sorrow turns into endless compassion.

Trust the heart.
Your amazing heart.
It transforms loneliness and feeling left out
into love, liberation, and new creation.

Peace is where the heart is.

Deep, abiding peace.

You are the Divine Feminine

You are the Divine Feminine.
Nothing can stop your full manifestation.

You live in all genders, in all races, in all beings
and you are the living presence in nature itself.

You are all powerful and you do not dominate by force.

Your truth, your beauty, your authenticity are self-sufficient.

What you love, you share
even when you remain in silence.

Your wholeness embodies all the opposites.
Your inclusiveness transcends everything.

You are not here in vain.
You are here to lessen everyone's pain.

Above all, you aspire to inspire everyone to their highest potential.

You do not give in to fear.
You always know
that your heart beats in unison with the cosmic heart.

When you speak or sing from your heart
deep healing takes place.

You do not know how to limit your love
and that is your strength.

Where there is love
miracles happen by themselves.

Love is the goddess of the earth

Love is everywhere — in the air, in the water,
in the snow, in the fire, in the bounty of the earth.
Can you feel love pulsating in you, now, and in all of existence?

You can open to love, step by step,
and also in one huge liberating explosion of life energy.

What could be more important than loving?

Love is the reason you are here.

Love now.
Love always.

Meditating on love is inviting her, welcoming her,
embracing her, nourishing her, inhabiting her.

Love is the goddess of the earth.

True happiness is experiencing love as your identity and your reality.

Ideology devoid of love is sterile and doomed to fail.
Dedicate your practice to the happiness of all beings.

All beings, in their true nature, are aspiring to love
and want to share this love.

As the goddess of the earth love is inspiring you
to accomplish your part.

That this may manifest on this day of love
and during all your days on earth.

As love you do not know fear.
As love there is no death.
As love you fully live in this moment.

Be love.
Only love.

Connected through love,
you will always find your loved ones, again and again.

Peace. Love. Happiness.

Loyalty to your inner royalty

The angel of dignity wants to speak some words to you.

You are pure consciousness.
As consciousness no one can question your dignity.

Dignity is a form of loyalty.
Loyalty to your inner royalty.

Dignity is also a form of confidence, self-confidence.
You are confident about what you really are.

Can you give some meditative space now to your essence
so it can breathe and fully be?

Many people are living in deplorable circumstances.
You can lift their spirits by seeing them in their full dignity.

Love is inclusive.

Can you feel empathy and respect for the poor,
the hungry, the prisoner, the immigrant, the sick?

In an enlightened society, dignity for everyone is a given.

Breathe in dignity.
Breathe out dignity.

What you truly are is not limited in time or space.

When you meditate you are sitting on a throne of dignity.

You are not in a hurry.
You are savoring this moment.

You are the light.
You are the light in the world.
You are the light in all beings.

Stephen Hawking

In this moment, nothing separates you from the whole universe.

The present moment.
The present moment is all there is — always.

Present love is all there is.

Present gratitude is all there is.
It is the bridge from your heart to the cosmos.

What you are is outside of time.
The present moment lets you enter and experience this reality.

It is a sacred way.
It is the way of true love.

Here you can find yourself.
Not as a separate entity.
As the glorious totality.

In honor of Stephen Hawking, let yourself roam.
Let your mind and your heart roam throughout the universe
and expand and expand...

Expand into nothingness and into everything that is.

From your form into formlessness.

From the cells of your body into stardust.

"Dante: D.C. = Palladium... Minerve-Athêna, Référence aux Valeurs établies, Ave! J. Soós, 27/3/1992

From the Big Bang to Nadabrahma, the sound of the universe.

You are pure vibration sent from the bow of love into eternity.

As your presence on earth is needed, do not forget your cosmic origin.

Many kids are marching today to demonstrate the way of peace.
May the angels of love inspire them.

Holy Friday

Your deep longing is to be free.

Never sacrifice your innate freedom.

Free to be.

Free to be what you are.

Free to be the love you are.

Meditating is a process of letting go of what you are not.

Watch the many movements of the mind and do not get involved.

Watch like a hawk.

Watch how the ego wants to crucify you and the world around you.

Do not get involved.

Your spirit, your immortal spirit, cannot be crucified.

Meditating is watching, witnessing, observing —
always opening and opening some more.

No pressure from the past making you heavy.
No anxiety for the future.
This moment now becomes so holy.

Holy and safe.

On Holy Friday you can already celebrate your resurrection
as you are awakening in the consciousness of one.

Centered in the core of your being, holy bliss arises.
The bliss of full beingness.

Unio mystica.

So be it!

Hallelujah.

Courageous aspiration leads to manifestation

Invite your guides and your helpers to sustain you.

They are present with you in dimensions of a higher frequency.

They come especially to you during prayer, during meditation,
during invocation and during healing work.

Feel the fragrance of their presence.

You are different from them in form, not in essence.

They open your heart, if you let them.

Imagine that you are bowing to each other, in deep, mutual respect.

You care for the earth and you are concerned
for the quality of civilization on this planet.

Each being, each race, each forest deserves to be treated with dignity.

Your guides are explaining the significance of "the golden rule" —
treat others the way you want to be treated yourself.

The guides are reminding you why you came to earth.

The vision you came with.

Even as you sit in the vibration of these words,
the vision may come back to you.

Stay true to your vision.
It makes a big difference.

The world is in need of many more dreamers.

You are one of them and you want to support all of them — socially and energetically.

Allow for a new world order to arise
from the depth and the strength of your untamed heart.

Courageous aspiration leads to manifestation.

Angels of manifestation are blessing you.

Miracle of love

Can you feel the love that is here?

When you give your mind a chance to rest, you will feel it even more.

The miracle of love.
The miracle of benevolent change.

Love, as wisdom, has one burning question for you —What are you really?

Being with this question immediately elevates the quality of your consciousness.

You become conscious of a loving and a living presence in you and in all things.

It is this presence that allows you to be connected, deeply, with reality.

Connected like this you experience a peace
that has not been very prevalent in the history of humanity.

Could this peace be what you really are?

Ask love.
She will tell you.

Love as wisdom.
A divine partnership.

Wake up! Wake up!
It is easy.
What you are is your natural state.

Have trust, even though your home is burning.
You are part of a collective shift in consciousness.

Deep down you do know what you are.
Celebrate this knowing.

How may humanity ever learn?

Breathe in love.
Breathe out love.

Now you are in the center of the truth of what you are.

How may humanity ever learn?

The antidote to fear and violence
is listening to what love has to say.

Love has words of wisdom.
Love is the answer and the never-failing comfort.

No event can stop you from reaching for
and finding the peace within you.

United in this you are bonded
and supported in the oneness of love
and the beauty of your eternal being.

The vastness of your silence is a prayer
and cannot be misunderstood.

It embraces the whole globe
and mitigates the suffering.

You are the light in this world.
Your presence makes a radical difference.

What you are, you share.
Be love.

With every trigger, with every challenge
love renews its invitation
to be what you are.

Spring Equinox

The promise and the pledge of Spring Equinox.

In an intelligent and benevolent universe, new creation is always welcomed.

On planet Earth, all its creatures still respond very deeply to Nature's cycles.

On this most auspicious day, what is your deepest longing
for your life and for life on this earth?

Are you willing
for the infinite heart of wisdom and compassion to guide you?

Do you have confidence that you have all the know-how you need?

Are you willing to greet the sun, the water, the air, Mother Gaia?

Are you willing to greet, in deep gratitude, what you were created for?

Do you see that greeting and gratitude
are the two wings of the infinite heart?

When you see all this, you are well on your way
to celebrate this day.

Every act of kindness, every act of forgiveness,
visible or invisible, makes a difference.

Just as you are, on some level, the entire universe is very aware of everything.

Open-mindedness, in service of open-heartedness,
can take all the barriers down
between you and complete freedom.

Summer Solstice

Summer Solstice — there is precious magic in the air.

A most auspicious time to meditate and to perform sacred rituals.

To charge the batteries of your body and your spirit.

Invoke the sun for courage and self-mastery.

Pray for the perception of a vision.

A vision for yourself and for the world.

A vision for the children, for the refugees, for those who are oppressed.

See yourself riding on the back of a white buffalo
into the blazing light of this vision.

The ascended masters are helping you.

You have a brave heart.
You are the rainbow warrior.

Today, all over your beautiful planet, seekers of truth, like yourself,
are gathering to enhance the presence of light and love.

You are the light you seek.

Receive the light now in your third eye center.
Not just from the sun.
From many, many galaxies.

Halloween and Samhain

The angel of truth, the angel of mercy
and the angel of compassion are here with you.

As you meditate,
listen to their questions and suggestions.

The first question —
What is the reality of your experience, in this moment?

No pressure.
Take your sweet time with this.

What is the reality of your experience, in this moment?

Can you observe this without any trace of judgment?

Can you observe with curiosity and passion?

Can you observe and distinguish between your thoughts and feelings —
always coming and going like the airplanes in the sky —
and the sacred presence which never leaves you?

Witnessing all this is a tool for self-empowerment.

It gives you space for pause and inner peace.

It is the secret of self-enquiry.
Just checking where you are, right now,
and what you always are, right now.

It is the perfect season for introspection.

Today is Halloween and Samhain, the Celtic festival,
marking the end of the harvest and the beginning of winter.

It is the powerful fire time in between Fall Equinox and the Winter Solstice.

Absorb as much cosmic light as you can
and balance it with the teachings of shadow.

It is the time to light candles in memory and mourning of the souls
that have departed, the recent ones and the more ancient ones.

It is also the Eve of All Saints.

Receive the wisdom teachings of your spiritual ancestors.

Right now, your most potent spiritual practice
is to temper the fire of hate with the water of your love.

Open your hearts to all the people in oppression and in danger.

You cannot, in good faith, turn your back on a caravan of despair.
If you do, you are betraying yourself.

Send your prayers.

Remember St. John of the Cross.

Sometimes a person passes through a dark night of the soul.
Sometimes a country does.
Sometimes the world does.

The angel of truth, the angel of mercy, the angel of compassion are helping.

They are bowing to you in deep respect for your understanding.

Light and darkness.
You are eternal witnessing.

You are very resourceful

You are very resourceful.

And love is very resourceful.
If you let her.
If you let her be.

She always wants to take you to freedom.

Freedom, true freedom, is foremost an inner affair.

Knowing this is a giant step forward in your development.

It starts with a glimpse of insight that this is the case.

Through your steadfast commitment and by grace,
this becomes your lived reality.

Under the law of grace, you can experience
that even a mishap is turned into a blessing.

Everyone deserves love.

It is a basic human right.

When it seems you have fallen out of grace,
a network of friendship and support, however small,
can pull you out of despair.

And naturally you can trust
that from the world of spirit
support is coming to humanity
and to you in particular without any interruption.

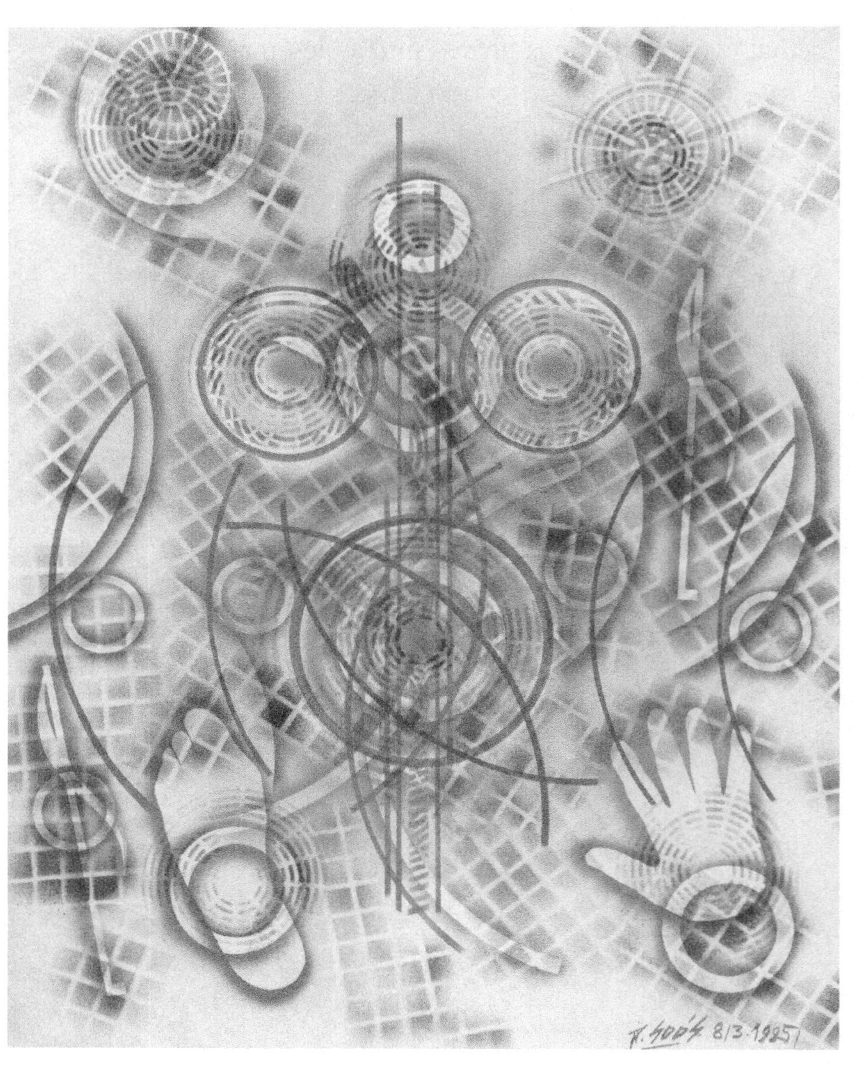

CHAPTER 2

Conscious Beingness

To be or not to be, that is the question.

Even people who have never read or seen anything by William Shakespeare are probably familiar with this famous line from *Hamlet*.

All the Inspired Guidances, in one way or another, try to guide the listener or reader into experiencing the relevance of this question. Here I have grouped those meditations that feature this line of inquiry.

In everyone's life there are moments of conscious beingness. Moments when you are aware that something— through you — is consciously perceiving what is present in and around you. Those moments can offer themselves unexpectedly and do not have to be extravagant. They often take place in the so-called "mundane reality." They can take you to your core and make a lasting impression on you.

I give a simple example from my own life, when my parents came to visit Kathy and me in Oregon. I, along with my two brothers, had offered them this trip as a surprise for their 60th wedding anniversary. They needed a bit of encouragement to undertake the journey; they were already well into their eighties and the cross-Atlantic flight from Europe to the West Coast had become fatiguing. It was their sixth and last visit to us, and in the end they were very happy with it.

While Kathy was seeing her clients in our home, I first took my parents for a week to our beautiful coast to relax, to enjoy and to recover. On the second day my mother fell asleep after lunch.

I am alone now in the presence of my father, which I know may not happen much anymore.

My Dad is reading a book, as am I. We are sitting next to each other on the balcony of our condo, overlooking the magnificent Pacific Ocean. As a matter of fact, I am waiting and wanting, as often happens, to exchange something of a deeper nature with him and I don't know how to get it started. Also, I do want to disturb his reading.

All of a sudden, his book is finished. I see him watching the coming and going of the waves. I can sense that deep inside he is really very still and content. He feels that his life has been good, and he has been grateful for this for quite some time now. He also enjoys my company and finds it easier to relate to Mom when I am around. Especially here, undisturbed, in the presence of the peace and beauty of the Pacific.

My father never took a meditation class. That was never part of his path. He did love to spend hours in his garden to quietly tend to his roses. The loft he built in his home became another sanctuary and refuge where he would paint for long stretches of time.

There we are, both still sitting at the ocean. Without saying anything, I allow his present beingness to take me into a more and more open space. All my needs and expectations are vanishing into the limitlessness of the space. Beingness is enveloping father and son in a moment of inexplicable and unforgettable grace.

The golden key

Here is the golden key.
Your commitment to stay present in each moment as it is occurring
initiates you into an authentic way of being.

This commitment is voluntary.
When you make it and when you apply it
there is an immediate effect.

Your energy field is no longer draining itself.
It is simultaneously relaxed and very alive.

When you experience this as a group
the mechanisms of falling asleep are being replaced
by an eagerness to explore the more brilliant aspects of reality.

Can you see right now that your inner space
is far more luminous than outer space?

Can you feel that your heart is beating in perfect unison
with the uniqueness of this moment?

When you surrender to this moment
you are ready and available for the next moment.

Be aware of the profound simplicity of this practice.
The less you do, the more you are.

This is your natural state.
It is fully awakened, right now.

Each moment a new invitation to recommit to being present.

The path of joy

Always remember
— this time you are voluntarily choosing the path of joy.

On this path you are a loving friend to yourself.

On this path you enjoy going inside
and finding vast, open space.

On the way, not avoiding anything,
you come upon openness after openness.

Your heart is the guide.
Your open mind is the happy servant.

Such a journey cannot fail.
There is no agenda.
There is no attachment.

States of mind come and go.
Awareness of what you really are
grows, moment by moment.

This awareness is not individual.
It shares itself, simultaneously, with everyone.

This presence, this unobstructed presence,
is not bothered by mind chatter and feelings of inadequacy.
This presence is joy itself and it is you.

Widen your horizon

First, widen your horizon, in all directions,
including the space above the crown.

In a second movement, invite the alive presence of your innermost being.

Can you observe that your innermost being
is immediately aware that you are turning to it?

You could see it as your sacred friend
who has been trying to guide you
from one lifetime to another lifetime,
from one form to another form.

One more step — loosen your attachment to any form
and find the formidable freedom of the formless.

You are in all things
All things are in you.

New creation is able to take birth in you and take root in you.

The dominant feeling is the joy and gratitude to be with the Absolute.

This is the great adventure.
It is Love seeking and finding Love.

The adventure has chosen you.
Your heart is saying: "Yes, this is what I am and this is why I am."

The light of your essence

May you be in touch now with your essence.

Aware of your essence, you are remarkably stable
even in the midst of storm and strife.

Nothing can rob you of your essence.
At the most, you can be forgetful of it.
Inner quiet makes your essence shine forth.

Your essence is undivided and fearless and sees love always —
whether it is hiding or not.

Happiness arises again and again
when you realize that your essence resides outside of time and space.

Duality is being stuck in one of the opposites.
Non-duality is ascending into oneness embracing everything.

Your essence is formless.
It experiences no need to defend itself.

The light of your essence is not of this world.
It reaches into you from the beyond.

Walk gently on the Earth

As a human being, you have the wonderful capacity
to focus your awareness.

You can even be aware of awareness itself.

Just as an experiment
bring your awareness now to the earth underneath you
and consider it as a very sacred spot.

In the meantime, you are aware of all the sounds around you
and all the sensations in you.

See yourself now as a majestic and ancient tree.

With deep, deep roots in the earth
and a very tall spine all the way into the sky.

Almost no thoughts are stirring in you.
You are so very tranquil.

The tree is sharing its essence with you —
its presence, its strength, its good-naturedness.

Receive through the tree all the nourishment you need
and give it back your appreciation and your tenderness.

Allow the presence of Nature to feed you.
It reminds you of your own natural goodness.

Walk gently on the Earth.
Be aware of every step.
It is a way into happiness.

Source

Source can never go out of existence.
Neither can the real you.

Knowing this as a very deep intuition
finishes the tyranny of fear.

Peace

May peace descend on you, deep abiding peace.

Such peace does exist, beyond your emotions,
beyond the many movements of the mind.

You are experiencing it for yourself
as you are turning the totality of your attention inward.

You are discovering the sacred space
that has been fully yours
before your body came into being.

Your body has a visceral memory
of its own creation and organic development
according to divine plan.

Peace is there, and purpose, and harmony
and a connection to Source that is very pure.

Peace prevails when your body, mind and spirit
are felt and understood as a sacred alliance.

As the benediction of peace descends
it gracefully restores your cells
to the full potential of their original blueprint.

Truth

Can you hear the truth?
Your heart can.
Truth is the home of the heart.

Since ancient times the masters of wisdom have proclaimed
that truth is not hidden from you,
at least not on purpose.

They say that the sincerity of your search
delivers truth directly on your doorstep.

For express delivery
investigate first what you are and what you are not,
where you are and where you are not.

Are you your body
or are you rather that which is aware of your body?

Are you a limited personal entity
or are you rather that which transcends all this?

Are you in the world or is the world in you?

Can you see that each vantage point creates its own reality?

There is a moment when all these questions have fulfilled
their purpose.
Now you simply are the eternal truth of what you are.

The miracle never stops

This is the miracle.
There is so much divine light in you at all times.

Are you willing to see this light?
To acknowledge it and let it shine?

You must be willing
since no one else can make it shine for you.
This constitutes your freedom.

Real freedom is to be consciously this light
as you pursue your sacred destiny moment by moment.

Very auspiciously you took birth once again
to fulfill the beauty of this destiny.

In this you are entitled to seek support.
Existence is aware of your commitment to truth and love
and will supply the help you need.

Your task is to recognize the form in which this help is showing up.

The miracle never stops.
As you focus on the inner light it grows, expands and multiplies.

This light cannot die.
It is beyond form.
It creates, sustains and renews all things and all beings
and it is not part of time.

The Divine

Regardless of how you are feeling right now
this is the perfect time to surrender to the Divine.

Just having this as an intention changes the atmosphere
inside you and all around you.

The Divine is very much aware of your meditating and praying
and is responding to you as a harmonious wave washing over you.

Each wave reminds you of your love essence.

The dolphins, the whales, all the spirit animals
find it very easy now to commune with you.

For millions of years you were part of the sea yourself,
part of the mountains, of the forests.
All these connections live in you.

As you reclaim all the manifestations of what you really are
you fully live in God.

Then, even earth has become a paradise
and your greatest joy is to share it.

Wherever you are, walk gently on the earth.
Each step, each breath, each thought is sacred.
As sacred as you are.

The sacred

Regardless of what is going on with you
physically, emotionally, mentally or spiritually
always remain open to receiving the rewards
of communing deeply with the sacred.

The sacred is not far away.
It is very near.
It also resides inside of you.
It reveals itself in every single heartbeat.

Such love, such compassion and such tremendous
tenderness.

This is the Grail of all seeking.
Never stop until it finds you.

To be aware of its permanent closeness is a great advantage.
No need to get lost in the many distractions.

The sacred is in the eye of the beholder,
in the peace and the emptiness of the meditator.
It is in all things and all beings at all times.

The noise of the world cannot deafen it.
It shares its light indiscriminately and abundantly.

You who know yourself as the sacred
have come home and will never be lost again.

Attention

There is a very obvious and very beautiful spiritual rule:
Pay more attention to this moment
than to any other moment.

This immediately engages the fullness of your being.

Your being is comfortable with silence.
It lives in what is.
It hears the call of the raven, the sound of the rain,
the intimacy of everything that is.

When you keep paying attention
you may notice that the love you are seeking
is actually holding you.

If it helps you
you can also whisper to yourself, "I am this love."

Embracing the truth of what you are
is an act of love.
It brings your surroundings into harmony.

This moment.
Always this precious moment.
Unwrapping, in wonder, the gift of this moment.

The cosmic orchestra

The most wonderful gift to yourself
is to allow plenty of room in your heart
to receive the embrace of your true nature.

To facilitate this, you could invoke
any image of the Divine that touches you,
any guide or teacher you feel close to,
or any unity experience that has ever come to you.

One more step may prove to be useful —
gently suggest to your "little me," the me of the personality
to recede in the background
and invite the love that you are
to fully occupy the foreground.

Now, truly, you are standing on solid ground.
You are connecting to eternity
and you know with certainty
that what you have been searching for
is this reality, the reality of what you are.

You never have to leave from here.
If you feel lost, accidentally, just be willing
to retrace these steps.

Healing continues to take place on so many levels
as you cherish your identity as love.

Now, as a finely tuned instrument
you are playing your perfect part in the cosmic orchestra.

Do yourself a great favor

Do yourself a great favor
and set all your worries to the side.
Really, all of them.

Now surrender your heart to love.
Invite divine presence to reveal to you
the mystery of your true self.

Your true self is not bound by the limitations
of time or space.

It was there before your body formed itself.
It will be there after the dissolution of your body.
It is there right now.

Some saints or sages are so strongly established in this self
that there seems to be a shining halo around them.
In essence, your true self is not different at all.

As you are yielding to this,
as it is taking over,
there is a combined sense of deep love, peace, power,
spaciousness
and a tremendous humbleness in the face of the mystery.

It is part of your training to learn how to live from this place.

Even though you are stepping into unknown territory
something in you already knows this is the way to go.

Nothing else makes much sense.
Love is the way to be.

Know that this is the truth about you.

What are you?

What are you — really?
This line of inquiry leads you most directly to Source.

It establishes you in your true identity,
in the timeless, the absolute, the unknowable.

It liberates you from feeling confined in your body,
or in the world, for that matter.

What are you really?
The ancient sages and the modern sages asked this question.
Buddha asked it. Jesus did.
Ramana Maharshi suggested it all the time —
to be with this question, to live it.

This question opens you up, both directly and steadily,
to the light within.

Unity is reality

While on earth, be as fully on the earth as you can
without giving up the memory of your full potential as a cosmic being.

As you claim your potential
you are no longer needy.
You are freer than ever.

As all the root systems in the forest interconnect
so does the consciousness of the heart.
Separation is illusion.
Unity is reality.

Witnessing whatever arises

Witnessing whatever arises within you,
without a trace of judgment,
is a very blessed state.

It gives you a solid anchor in the Now.
In a way, you become the Now.

Witnessing is not an activity of the mind.
It is an unobstructed state of consciousness.

You see through the veils of illusion
into the brilliance of your true reality.

Habitual perception of lack and limitation
is replaced now by an awareness of abundance and perfection.

Naturally, in this way, a deep peace descends on you,
love freely runs through you
and you have a sense of the inherent oneness of all creation.
You just know that this is so.

Witnessing is resting in being,
forever and always in this moment.

Witness the eternal,
the absolute, in you and as you
and you are free.
Now!

The radiant Self

The radiant Self.

It is always in deep silence.
It has no limitations.

It makes itself known to you each time you invite it.

The practice of inviting your radiant Self, which is your real Self,
for longer stretches of time, is called meditation.

Mental suffering cannot survive
in the presence and under the protection of the real Self.

Joy, kindness, gratitude, optimism flourish
in the embrace of the radiant Self.

The more you love yourself
the more you will seek out the company
of this very best of friends.

Sometimes you may wonder how to surrender.
Be with your real Self.
It is always in a state of surrender.

Loving arising out of being

Can you just very simply allow yourself to be?

The guidelines for meditating are easy enough.
You are willing to witness and to watch.
Willing to be present and awake.
Willing to be in the flow.
All this in a very relaxed way.

Thoughts and feelings are not treated as your enemies.
They are welcomed and released
in one spontaneous movement.

The beauty of your meditation
comes from the respect and reverence
for the mystery of what you are and what life is.

Somehow you are here
and somehow you discover that your happiness resides
in the immediacy of this moment — with an open heart.

When you share heart space with yourself
you are more willing to include others as well.

Loving arising out of being is one ongoing sharing.

Your gratitude will never cease

Can you acknowledge how precious this moment is?

Each time you can
you receive a very sweet taste of your liberation.

Liberation cannot be bought or sought.
It can be recognized, however, in this very moment,
as your eternal and innermost state.

Meditating on this and as this
often produces an immediate bliss.

Enjoy this.
It is very beautiful and very real.
And never get stuck in this.

Your greatest opportunity, often very challenging,
is to take this with you, wherever you are, in all your relations.

Letting go, surrendering and forgiving.
This is the holy trinity of your practice.

When you want to do this,
unseen forces come to you to help you.
This discovery creates a new life for you,
full of grace and wonder.

You are not alone.
The ancient sages had knowledge of this pathless path,
the direct path, always available, right now, in this precious moment.

As you walk this path,
and why would you not?
your gratitude will never cease.

Your light

Your light is shining now, bright and steady,
a delight for all to see.

Your light is prior to that of the world.
It is ancient and eternal.

Mother Gaia

Take note.
A sense of the sacred descends in you
when you are willing to look at your true nature.

Listen carefully.
This is not difficult at all.
Shift your attention from that which is perceived
to that which is perceiving.

Such perceiving is seeing beyond duality.

It is allowing the reality of source
to become your reality.

The silence resulting from this is charged with freedom
and deep transformation.

One openness follows another openness....

In this openness everything is being honored, all beings,
including your unique manifestation.

Mother Gaia, ever giving, ever loving,
is honored for what she is.

Use this gift with gratitude.
In the clarity of real seeing
you have become more than a mere mortal.
You are immortal.

Living Light!

Living light!
Brilliant, living light is surrounding you.

Do not stop searching
until the brilliant light has firmly established itself
in your mind, in your body, and in your heart.

It is true, of course, that what you are searching for
is already residing inside of you
and yet, it has to be uncovered before it can fully manifest.

You who are passionate about this
are very often visited by grace.

Grace can flow through authentic teachers or teachings
and leads you to your inner light, your inner teacher.

Of the Buddha and the Christ, it is said
that they are beyond form and beyond the formless.
This is true too of the real you.

Living light, brilliant living light is surrounding you
and fully penetrating your mind, your body and your heart.

You are one now with Nadabrahma, the sound of the universe.

Om Shanti!
Om Shanti!
Om Shanti!

Open sky

Open sky, always expanding.
Big, beautiful, brilliant, bright.
You are that and you are even beyond that.

Clouds are passing by.
They come and they go.

Now, be aware, fully aware,
of that which never comes or goes.

Here lies your freedom.
Here lies your happiness.

Established in your true nature
you are honoring all forms, including your own
and you can send love to all beings.

Your biggest contribution to the world
is to allow your love light to shine
wherever you are.

The eternal dimension of what you are

The eternal dimension of what you are
is never far away.

It is the highest dimension of consciousness
and it is your supreme reality.

To be aware of this — first briefly, then steadily —
changes everything for you.

The idea that there would be a shortage of time
is replaced by the felt evidence that there is an ocean of timelessness,
for you and for everyone.

It relaxes you so deeply and so fundamentally.

This affects all your interactions, also with yourself.
There is more respect in them, more love, more soul.

While the eternity of your being is radiating its light
your actions in the world have clarity and demonstrate authenticity.

There is only one glorious journey.
It is both towards the light and always in the light.

No rushing, and no postponing either.
Savoring every single precious moment along the way.

Without discrimination or interruption
the eternal light is shining on everyone and everything.

God

When God is seen, not as a person, or an entity
but as the real reality
living as love through all things and all beings,
planet earth can be a paradise.

Inner silence

Inner silence brings about inner seeing.

To see, to really see, is to be free.

How do you really see?
Through the Heart.

How does the Heart awaken?
By constant devotion to the Absolute.

In this way you disappear as a person
and you reappear as pure presence.

By definition the Absolute never leaves the here and now.

Neither do you, when you allow time to gently explode into eternity.

Held and nourished by the Absolute
every single moment is a gift.

Even on earth so many awakened masters
are sharing beautiful Heart space with you, all the time.

The presence

The presence is gathering.
It envelops you.
It strengthens you.
It softens your heart.

Here it is easy for you to see that most movements of the mind
are really repetitive and redundant.
Let them dissolve.

Presence brings in a different quality of consciousness.

It is based on the joy of just seeing, just being.

Judgment has left.
Appreciation has taken its place.

The authenticity of your happiness

Welcome to your true home.
Relax now fully into what you already are.

What you are is the great mystery.
It is impossible to describe it.
It is possible to experience it.

As a human you are aware of being conscious.
Meditation is the sacred circumstance
in which this capacity is being used
as your ongoing vehicle for self-realization.

Self-realization is living in gratitude
according to the maximum of your potential.

What you do and what you do not do
arise spontaneously, organically out of being.

Your loving, your helping, your being of service
is not a compulsion.
It comes from the authenticity of your happiness.

Meditating (1)

Meditating is shifting most of your attention
from the outer to the inner.
This always leads you to the light of Source.

One with Source, nothing can disturb you.

One with Source, your body is relaxed.
Your mind is peaceful.
Your spirit is tremendously uplifted.

In this sunny spot you are encouraged
to abandon any remaining traces of self-concepts
that are criticizing or minimizing you.

Here the healthy confidence of Holy Spirit may enter you
and open your eyes to the light.
Self-confidence is needed to embrace your beauty as a light being.

Meditating (2)

There is no goal in meditation.
A goal creates tensions.

There is willingness.
There is openness for the transformation to take place.

You cannot make this happen.
You can allow for this to happen.

The sincerity of your search takes you home,
not just one time, a thousand times and more.
Now can be one of those auspicious times.

Meditating (3)

Meditating is the very refined and noble practice
of surrendering to the reality of what is.

When this is your sincere intention
you will see, every single time,
that a significant shift takes place.

You are shedding the relentless burden
of excessive thinking
and opening your heart to being.

It is praying without asking for anything.

It is seeing that you are everything.

It is discovering your joy and your strength
in the fullness of the emptiness.

It is being the rain, being the sun, being the air and the earth and being the witness of everything.

It is being surrounded by a host of angels.

When there is no more meditator,
when there is no more effort
everything becomes very quiet.

A blessing of grace takes place.
Separation is no more.

The mystery

Because you are present the mystery is taking place.

It never fails.
When you meditate, at some point the limited you
spontaneously dissolves into the eternal you.

It can feel very familiar and intimate
since it is your natural state.

There is a wonderful sense of peace here
and love and belonging.
Yes, you do belong here.

Sometimes you have to travel far away to find such a place.
Also, always right here, under your nose, by turning inward
and seeing what you really are...

In your natural state, totally relaxed and totally at ease,
the whole universe appears in you.

You are beyond the coordinates of time and space.
You are absolutely free.

<u>**A love without any motives**</u>

Gently relax now.
See yourself sitting on top of a magnificent mountain
and absolutely nothing is bothering you.

Thoughts of limitation are being replaced by thoughts of happiness.

Every so often there are no thoughts at all.

This is amazingly liberating.
It allows you to drop into beingness.

Beingness becomes inter-beingness.
It is emptiness and fullness.

It is a very deep feeling of connectedness
and a profound knowing of oneness.

In this place, which for any human being is the only true place
it is impossible to have enemies from your past or in your present.

Visiting this place is very healing.
Here your love arises naturally, spontaneously.

It is a love without any motives.
This makes it so transformative.

Steeping in the goodness of your own being
you disappear as a person
and you reappear as pure heart.

No more hiding

No more hiding.
No more seeking.
Embrace the totality of what you are.
It is beauty and love combined as one.

A dedicated devotee

You who have been a dedicated devotee for many lifetimes
are melting now, like butter in the blazing sun of Love.

Surrendering without any effort.
Disappearing, not leaving behind any trace.
Occasionally still repeating your last mantra:
"I am Love. You are Love. Love is All."

One sacred moment.
One taste.
One glimpse.
Love is not the prisoner of time.
Neither are you.

Beingness

Beingness.
Nothing radiates like beingness.
Here is the ending of your psychological pain.

Beingness is divine love
and it makes no distinctions whatsoever between the various beings.

Regardless of your circumstances you are being invited
personally and directly to enter into this love.
To know this and to experience it, this changes everything.

The self-treatment and the sharing of Reiki
are very respectful forms to transmit this love.

Love has no goal.
It seeds itself where it finds fertile ground.

Listen.
You are the sweetly singing seed of the new earth.

A message of love

Here is a message of love:
Your thoughts are creating the world.
What would happen if you knew
that you are divine perfection
as you are right now, this moment?

Experiment with this perception.
No longer will you look for approval or outside validation.
You will rest in your true self where all is well.

Silence then becomes the most intimate of friends.
You are connected to every blade of grass,
every ray of the sun, every drop of rain.
You *are* and that is enough.

Love is what you are.
What a great mantra to use:
I am love, I am love.
Until all the cells of your body
are repeating this in unison
and you can relax because you know that this is so.

I am love, I am love.
This you say to yourself.
You are love, you are love.
This you say to anybody you meet or think of.

Then a brilliant sun will awaken your mind,
open your heart, and change the world.

Blessing upon blessing

Completely present in the moment
blessing upon blessing comes to visit you.

The greatest blessing is your awareness of the presence
that accepts all that is without a trace of judgment.

The presence that supports everything and everyone
to find peace within themselves and within the universe.

Such love animates this presence.
It is the same love that animates you.
You really are this love.

It would not hide from you.
Why would it?
It is here now.

It looks for openness
and when it finds it, it pours itself into it.

Each time you breathe consciously, you become this openness.
You become the lungs of the collective aspiration.

Yes to this moment

Would you be willing to say yes to this moment?

The freshness, the delicacy, the uniqueness of this moment.

All the sensations present in this moment.

And you as the presence in which all of this appears.

No desire to run away from what is.

This is the way.
The way of peace and harmony,
even and especially when things are hard.

As you experiment with this
life walks towards you
in a big and loving embrace.

You find beauty in the ordinary.
You see the miraculous in the mundane.

The unborn Atman

Most blessed and fortunate are you
who are aware of the radiant light of your innermost being.

Established as the purity of this light
what could possibly happen to you?

A similar light shines from that which guides you,
which loves you, which accepts you unconditionally,
with all your gifts and all your shadow pieces.

You have worked very hard to reach this point in your development.
Do not stop here.
Rest, certainly, and always relax as best you can
and continue until eternal peace is yours.

Self-realization is the highest curriculum currently available on your planet.
Your life circumstances, your relations, your hardships, your joys
are helping you to master this curriculum.

When you meditate, your mind and body are relaxing.
The compassionate heart takes over.
A new configuration comes into being.

There is plenty of love for everyone.
This you will discover as soon as you give yourself permission
to love yourself.

The unborn Atman, that which you have always been, shines brightly.

Limitless Light

It is here.
Always.
Limitless Light.
Limitless Light.

Throughout your body, throughout your being.
Throughout the entire universe.

Nadabrahma — the sound of the universe.

Can you hear it? Humming. Through every single cell.

Leading you beyond the self-imposed limitations
into openness, vastness, happiness.

This is your true reality.

Limitless Light. Limitless Light.

As above, so below.

There it is. In the silence of the heart.

In the ear that can hear, it is striking a resounding chord of cosmic peace.

You are the created and the creator.
You are love, always embraced by the Beloved.

You are humble and that honors you.
You are powerful and that helps you.

You are.

Living Limitless Light.
Very, very beautiful living limitless light.

The absolutely astonishing light of your being

The absolutely astonishing light of your being!

There is nothing in the world that can prevent you
from experiencing the light of your being.

There is nothing inside of you that can prevent you
from seeing, accepting and declaring the light of your being.

The easiest entrance is always through the heart.

You have done this many times before.
You know how to do it now.

The distance between forgetting and remembering what you are is very tiny.

Be compassionate with yourself.
It is inevitable to forget.
It is a great joy to remember again.

Between forgetting and remembering there is one trustworthy bridge —
the love in your heart.

Know that this love is always present in the astonishing light of your being.

Whether they are aware of it or not, this is true for all beings.

Declaring your light, at least to yourself, blesses the world.

Nowhere to go.
The light is always here.

Here you have no name, no gender, no race, no nationality.

Here you are always free.

Affirming your right and your ability to be free.

The silence is so deep, as you remember the astonishing light of your being.

I Am All That I Am

Let your inner light shine.

All the mystics agree —
there are no adequate words to describe your union with all that is.

Even so —
what they say can soften and sweeten the landscape of your heart.

The mystic Rumi says:
You are a diver.
Your body just a heap of clothes left at the shore.
You are a fish whose way is through water.

Listen to your inner teacher.
He or she tells you this:
Just one glimpse of what you are and... everything changes.

You know that there is a deeper meaning to life.

You know you have a place on earth and among the stars.

You know that nobody can deny the truth of your experience.

This new knowing supports you in the easy times and in the difficult times.

It steers your life in directions you could not have anticipated.

Rational calculation is replaced
by the intelligence and the unexpectedness of love.

Rumi also says: *Love is the water of life.*

Your body is mostly composed of water.

Let your life flow to where it wants to.

One glimpse of your inner light is enough.

Let it shine!

Let love and light be your inner teacher.

A glimpse of light, right now, as you relax and meditate.

It can happen any moment when your heart and mind are at peace.

Say to yourself: I am light. I am love. I am peace.

Light I am.

Love I am
Peace I am.
I Am All That I Am

CHAPTER 3

The New Age and a Call for Action

THE INSPIRED GUIDANCES IN this section have a tone of urgency about what is happening on planet Earth at this moment. There is a sense that to sit passively at the sidelines cannot be an appropriate position — that it could even be a form of spiritual bypassing.

There are reminders that the New Age has actually started, that we are witnessing a shift in consciousness, and that empathy and social justice are more important than ever.

In the Guidances, "New Age" is used in the same way as the "Aquarian Age," based on astrological predictions that humans are entering an era of expanded consciousness. Personally, I remember how Jóska Soós would use these terms with such enthusiasm. I also resonate deeply with Eckhart Tolle as he points out in *A New Earth* that collective human consciousness and life on our planet are intrinsically connected: "*A new heaven*" *is the emergence of a transformed state of human consciousness, and 'a new earth' is its reflection in the physical realm.*"

This brings me to my most esoteric connection with the term "New Age" as it is conceived in the work of Sri Aurobindo, The Mother and Mother Meera. They could see clearly that in the current age, "supramental consciousness" would bring about a decisive change in the evolution of the earth consciousness. Mother, in particular, emphasized quite a while ago that everything that had been able to hide itself would be brought to the surface — and to the light — by the supramental. She said,

> *It is this artificiality, this insincerity, this complete lack of truth that appeared so shocking to me that ... one wonders how, in a world as false as this one, we can arrive at any truthful evaluation of things.*
>
> *But instead of feeling grieved, morose, rebellious, discontent, I had rather the feeling of what I spoke of at the end: of such a ridiculous absurdity that for several days I was seized with an uncontrollable laughter whenever I saw things and people! Such a tremendous laughter, so absolutely inexplicable (except to me), because of the ridiculousness of these situations." (Mother's Agenda Volume 1)*

Many of these Guidances call us to action, and to awareness of the state of the biosphere — heartfelt pleas to have respect for all beings. There are reminders that many of us are able to provide some healing. Some Guidances specifically refer to Reiki, since I often teach this particular form of healing.

My point of view is informed by books like the following: first, *Half-Earth: Our Planet's Fight for Life*, by the highly respected biologist Edward O. Wilson, who combines his vast scientific knowledge with a profound humanistic intelligence. In the prologue he writes, *"For the first time in history a conviction has developed among those who can actually think more than a decade ahead that we are playing a global endgame."*

Because of human activity on earth, the rate at which living species are disappearing is a thousand times higher than before the appearance of humans. This is a terrible disaster for life as we have known it. Wilson addresses the moral question: Will we continue to degrade the planet to satisfy our own immediate wants and needs, or will we find a way to halt the mass extinction for the sake of future generations?

Another book, *The Hidden Life of Trees: What They Feel, How They Communicate — Discoveries from a Secret World,* is by the German forester, Peter Wohlleben. How interesting that his name, in German, literally means "to live well." His book became the number one bestseller of non-fiction in Germany in 2015. On each page you can feel his love for trees and the forest. But there is more. He tells us riveting and true stories about the unexpected capacities of trees and presents the science to make sense of it all. Trees in a forest are very comparable to human families. They communicate with each other and constantly support each other's growth. Every tree is valuable to the community. Even strong trees get sick over the course of their lives. When this happens, they depend on their weaker neighbors for support.

I highly recommend both these books.

As you might recall, it is my good fortune to teach at Breitenbush Hot Springs in Oregon, which has been a First Nations village site for perhaps thousands of years. Whenever I am there — disconnected from phone, Wi-Fi, and electrical smog — bathing in the natural mineral pools, I become replenished and rejuvenated. In the summer of 2017, a forest fire which could easily have destroyed all the buildings on the property came close to its boundaries. Blessedly, the rains arrived just in time to turn the tide.

In the old growth forest, it is possible to hike and find enormous trees who have fallen down long ago and are now functioning as a habitat for many colonies of small, new life.

A couple of years ago while teaching a Reiki class there, I met a Japanese researcher. Her specialty is to capture the humming, or music, of trees. She puts electrodes on their branches to register vibrations, and also uses a computer program that translates them into "human" electronic music. Many of us had a chance to listen to this with headphones, and everyone was deeply moved. And then there was this....

On the Breitenbush property there are very few moving vehicles, especially in the area the scientist was studying. One day a piece of heavy machinery passed close to a tree. The tree immediately stopped humming. Dead silence ensued for about half an hour before the tree started humming again!

At another moment, a small group of my students and I started to give Reiki to one of her trees. Its sounds became even more beautiful and harmonious. When more people gathered around the tree, there was almost a sense of "disturbance" or "overwhelm," as we discerned by listening later through headphones. Just an hour later we resumed our Reiki practice of laying on of hands in our class. The consciousness, sensitivity and music of the trees brought our work to an even finer dimension.

What a very special world we live in! We are being asked to be very open and discerning. Sensitive and engaged. And especially, to *listen* for what could be our task or contribution, and to then find appropriate ways to implement it. The good news is that there is a constant stream of inspiration doing its very best to reach us from the invisible dimensions. I hope that the following Guidances will help with the fine tuning.

Atlantis

Souls incarnate in groups
and are here to learn successive lessons.

The general lesson bears repeating:
You are not the body.
You are not the mind.
You are the consciousness
that is able to perceive the body and the mind.

Often a reorientation takes place in your life
as you investigate this proposition.

For this witnessing consciousness, death is not so daunting.
It is a transition, most likely an initiation,
and probably a continuation.

This time the world is learning very specific lessons:
to share resources willingly,
to listen to all points of view,
to forgive oneself and others,
and to open oneself to healing and transformation.

You have a place in this.
The members of your soul group are encouraging you,
and the choices you make touch the lives of many.

It would be senseless to repeat Atlantis.
The opening of the heart is the greatest miracle.

Om Shanti.

When the elders are failing the young ones

Your teachers are here and would love to awaken your inner teacher.
Listen carefully.

Freedom of thought.
Freedom of speech.
And then your greatest freedom — the freedom to discover what you really are.

See yourself surrounded by the snowy mountain peaks of the Himalayas.

Suddenly you are merging with Buddha consciousness,
with Christ consciousness, with the consciousness of oneness.

Oneness with love.
Oneness with truth.
Oneness with the beauty and the sensitivity of the biosphere.

Having experienced oneness, you want to protect and to safeguard.

It is natural to protect what you fall in love with.

To protect what you took for granted for so long.

Democracy, mental sanity, ethical decency — where are they now?

Where is justice?
Where is social empathy?

Where is the art of listening, the art of statesmanship and stewardship?

When the elders are failing the young ones,
they in their turn are empowered to step forward with vision and clarity.

Spiritual practice, all across the globe, is a place
where great minds meet to receive insights based on love, peace and justice.

In the great open space of emptiness and effortlessness the divine speaks to you.
Trust what you receive.

Keep discovering what you are and appreciate what you are.

Everyone deserves respect

There are many beings who have taken vows to always support you.

They are very present to you when you are meditating.

Meditating contributes to peace —
to your inner peace and to peace in the world.

Seemingly, no one can solve the problems in the world.

And yet, and yet... your contribution is absolutely necessary and valuable.

Your kindness, your love, your open heart cannot be overestimated.

Equally crucial is respect.

Deep respect and dignity for all beings is the highest priority.

Everyone deserves respect.
You do.
The earth certainly does.
The downtrodden do.

The world as you know it now is but one choice among many.

From deep respect a new and much brighter world is able to arise.

Intention always precedes creation.

Meditation alone or together is new creation.

Experience how millions of neurons and cells are making fresh connections.

This is the power of true love.

United in love, everything — literally everything — is possible.

Never tolerate abuse of power.

Stand united in the love that you know and experience as true.

Beings of light and love are eternally grateful for your contribution.

As you pledge to respect this sacred earth,
you are awakening into a new reality.

The Aquarian Age

Simply and very delicately direct your undivided attention
to the core of your being.

It is so close, so intimate.
Closer even than your heartbeat.
More intimate than your breathing.

Some refer to it as the arms of the Beloved.

It is so vast.
It tolerates no restrictions.

Going in this way
first and foremost allows you to go
everywhere and anywhere.

There is such magnificence here,
eternal loving, embracing and celebrating.

May all beings experience this happiness and tenderness.

May all beings find their way home.

May all beings find their way to each other.

The silent transmission from heart to heart
is the real revolution of the Aquarian Age.

The rainbow beings

Your beauty, your love, even your perfection
are already abundantly here.
Can you see that this is so?

Now you are being offered the simplicity of the master key —
embrace this very moment, including your perfect presence in it.

This key is designed to work in all situations.

True self-love brings about a genuine and deep appreciation for all beings.

Yes, all beings.
The rainbow beings, beings of the mountains, of the trees,
the rocks, the animals and the minerals, the stars and the planets.

In silent contemplation it is evident.
You are one with everything.

A new dawn is upon you.
More and more members of the human species
are reporting on this as the reality of their own experience.
Trust it.
The effects of this are far reaching and irreversible.

Your ancient ancestors are here

Your ancient ancestors are here.
They love and care for you.

They are very aware of your struggles and challenges.
They do see your potential.
They want to safeguard your future.

Their message to you is simple.
Love is the key and you can always find it
in the beauty and purity of your heart.

This is how you use the key:
You develop a loving and conscious connection with this moment.

In this moment the present and the past and the future
are intersecting each other — also, all realities, all dimensions.

Each open heart, each dedicated spiritual center
is a portal to higher consciousness.

Connect now your heart with your third eye and with your crown
and let the light shine.

This light feeds you and renews you.

In this light you are placing your dream for the earth.

It is a dream for all beings, all peoples,
all species on the earth and beyond the earth.

When you realize how much love there is for you,
you only have one wish — to share this love.

And trust that in your silent meditation
this dream is being rooted on earth.

You are the dream and the dreamer, you are creation and the creator,
you are love and the lover.

You are visiting earth right now
to participate in the great turnaround.

Everything you are and everything you can be
is needed and will be used.

May peace embrace you.

The One manifests as the many

The One manifests as the many.
Since the beginning of time, many masters have come to visit here
to guide the development and evolution of human consciousness.
As they leave the earth plane
their light bodies are even more accessible
through your prayer and meditation.
It is a blessed benediction to enter into their field of radiance.

In your lifetime, the stream of Lord Buddha and Jesus the Christ
have finally merged as one.
Compassion, forgiveness and mindfulness are now seen as one revelation.

Mother India sends you Shankara, Ramana Maharshi,
Nisargadatta Maharaj, Babaji, Mirabai, Anandamayi Ma.
They are more alive than ever.

From Tibet comes the shamanic stream:
Padmasambhava, Marpa, Milarepa, Tilopa, Naropa.

Your lineage is not just genetic but is spiritual and extraterrestrial.
As you go into the One you become the many.

It is wise to claim all this as your heritage.
There is richness here and a depth of connection and a love
that can never be taken away.

The supramental light

Gather the supramental light inside of you.

This light wants to circulate through your body
and permeate it on the very fine level of the cells
so they can be renewed.

It is a formidable evolutionary force.

As it opens you, please welcome the possibility of self-realization.

Welcoming is a life-giving dynamic
that already points to the open nature of your true self.

Gratitude is a similar movement and expression,
especially the gratitude for what you really are
and always will be — pure love.

To take birth as your current form
has been a miraculous accomplishment.
To evolve into your next expression of love
is the great adventure of consciousness.

By pioneering and undertaking the transformation
on behalf of the collective
on occasion you will meet with tremendous resistance.
Stay the course.
Every opening, however small, leads to victory.

A grateful heart gives thanks
for the invitation to evolve
into ever more refined expressions of love.

Legacy

What legacy will you leave behind?
Let it be love and only love
for that is what you are.
To know that and live in that
is your goal and your current practice.
Welcome to such a splendid life!

When fear grips you in the gut
allow your belly to become soft
and call upon love as your ally.
Calamity turns into opportunity.

For years and even lifetimes
you have been working on yourself.
Now you are ready for the last step.
Replace all judgment with compassion,
all guilt with forgiveness,
and all fear with love.

Once you have set this intention
relax and surrender to what is.
Be the observer.
The observer and the observed are one.
You are one.

You are one.
The world is one.
Consciousness is one.
The power of one is the answer
to your planet's predicament.

Blessed are the ones who transcend duality
and remember oneness as the only reality.

Respect for yourself

With great respect for yourself
make a distinction between your mental reactivity
and divine presence in you.

Certainly, you can feel the energetic difference
between agitation and peace.

This enables you to speak your truth lovingly, clearly and succinctly.

Wonderfully committed as you are to the process of awakening
you become vigilant as to where you are taking direction from.

Asking sincerely.
Listening deeply.
Asking and listening as if you are a representative
for the sake of helping humanity
because that is what you are.

Humanity is at such a crossroads.
Divine Mother weeps for the children who are not safe
and pleads with you to follow the way of the heart.
There is no other way.

<u>The mystics, the shamans, the poets, the meditators</u>

Reality is one
and you have the freedom to experience it in many dimensions.

The dimension of the heart is by far the most absolute
as it transcends time and space.

Sacred beings of light have taken a pledge
to guide you into this most exquisite realm of the heart.
They are here now.

In a very relaxed way, and very simply, be available to their presence,
their input, their caring, their tremendous tenderness and their majesty.

Since reality is one, please understand that your love
is never separate from their compassion
and their eagerness to be of service.

Every year now, the veil between the dimensions is becoming thinner and thinner
so that love can freely flow without any boundaries.

Trust the reality of your experience.
Never stop exploring.
At the edges, happiness comes to meet you.

The mystics, the shamans, the poets, the meditators
have all received glimpses of the ultimate reality.
You are standing on their shoulders
and helping to open the portal for many others.

It is happening — together

Be careful with the multiple distractions
that can drain your life energy.
There is a way out.
Bring your undivided attention
to the sacredness and the eternity
of your real self.

What meets you here is mysterious and very life-giving.

It awakens a force in you that changes everything.

The centers in your body start to free themselves.

The anguish of some old mental formations dissolves
into the presence of what you really are right now.

Your heart is no longer timid.
It invites you into ever-new territory.

You are not alone.
At the right moment you meet somebody,
happy to walk with you.

How ingenious are the laws of creation.
By focusing on what is eternal in you
you can see what is right in front of you.

What guides you forward
is the unlimited intelligence of life itself.

Yield to it
and it takes you under its wing,
wherever you are,
wherever you go.

This kind of awakening is no longer for the happy few.
It takes place wherever there is sincerity of motivation.

Think lovingly of your brothers and your sisters
who would share this adventure with you.
It is happening — together.

Creating a benevolent field

Give some space to the sweet silence
that is always inside of you.

Almost immediately the effects are noticeable.
The tensions in the forehead are disappearing.
The heart is more open.
Your breathing is more regular.

Interior silence is able to accommodate many disturbances.

To deepen the silence
try the following excellent entryway.
Pay attention to the intervals in between your thoughts.

As you notice them, they tend to become longer and even longer.

It is a bit like having your foot in the door
and then it opens by itself.

Sacred silence overtaking you.

If it helps you
you could invoke the archetype of the meditating yogi
sitting for a long stretch in a luminous cave
or on top of a beautiful mountain
or under the protection of the Bodhi tree.

As you allow your inner silence to manifest
you are creating a benevolent field
in which many find peace and sustenance.

Never get stuck

Never get stuck.
Keep engaging with the sacred teachings of life.

Among the many teachers, Love is like the high priestess.
When in doubt ask yourself, "What would love do?"

Resisting Love is a form of resenting life.

Love blossoms beautifully in a climate of courage and curiosity,
surrender and acceptance.

Absolutely refuse to feel sorry for yourself.
Love transcends all that, in an instant.

You are Love.
Let this in till you know and feel that this is the truth about you

You are Love, even before the beginning of the beginning.

Knowing what you are stops the projection of separation.

You are Love.
The servant of the priestess and the priestess yourself.

To forget what you are is misery.

The life of your most glorious awakening

Let this be the life of your most glorious awakening.

Nothing is sweeter than the taste of your true nature.

As this is becoming the regular foreground of your attention
the real transformation has begun.

Old habits may still surface.
Do not be upset.
They are met now
by the loving awareness of your true nature
and they dissolve in its compassion.

This is the journey into the heart of your essence
and it has always been your destiny to take it.

It is the journey of becoming more and more empty
so that the whole universe can pour itself into you.

You will find many who want to walk or sit with you for a while.
Such company is inspiring and uplifting
and is a true fellowship.

You made it.
You are home now.

The spiritual warrior is a shape shifter

You are a spiritual warrior
as you are not afraid of your own vulnerability.

Longing and loneliness, love and gratitude,
felt through the heart, lead to awakening.

Nurture the soft spot you have for all creatures
and walk gently upon the earth.
Your practice does not condone harm
to yourself or others.

As a shaman, as a yogi, as a meditator,
as a mature human being
you accept life's challenges as teachings.

You celebrate everything, even inadequacy,
as a portal to perfection.

Nothing ever stays the same.
The spiritual warrior is a shape shifter.
When your form is open and flexible
your essence is unobstructed.

May your practice benefit all beings.
May your heart touch all creatures.
May your peace and silence bless the earth.

The archetype of the sacred warrior

From now on, many times a day, try to remember what you really are.
It will immediately stabilize you on earth and in heaven.
Notice how the archetype of the sacred warrior has been activated in you.
This warrior is committed to embracing the present moment.
This warrior loves nature and wants to protect it.

This warrior honors the inner wounds and wants to use them for transformation.
You are confident that your transformation contributes to the harmony in the collective.
This is why you live; this is why you love; this is why you do your inner work.
In the work, you find tremendous strength and you learn to appreciate deeply the help of others.
In this way you discover that there is divine order in all things, always, even in tiniest details.
As a sacred warrior, you are willing to love yourself unconditionally, and from this place to share your love with all beings, regardless of whether they can accept this or not.
Your ancestors are blessing your life, your work, your family and your friends, and are very aware of all your prayers.

Reiki (1)

Your purpose here is the journey into your heart.

Your heart is very beautiful as it is.
This is a good starting point.

Contractions around the heart are just habits based on fear.

Ask the angels of love and Reiki to gently touch your heart
until all contractions are dissolved and healed.

Healing is recognizing the one heart in all beings.

When you take this journey
every day of your life is full of meaning.

Those who travel with you become very dear to you.

You may see them or not; they are always with you.

The journey itself is the teacher

The angels of love and Reiki are still touching your heart
and through your heart, the heart of the world.

Reiki (2)

To love yourself brings about a deep relaxation.

A sense of well-being spreads through all the cells of the body.

To love and support each other
gives you tremendous trust in the goodness of existence.

Even with strangers, Reiki is a safe and sacred way to share your love.

When enough people dedicate themselves to love
a quantum leap in consciousness takes place.

Initiation promotes this leap.

At times you are this leap.

The angels of Reiki accompany you wherever you are.

Show gratitude for every living thing.

Reiki (3)

A deep stillness meets you
when you investigate the truth of what you are.

It is the stillness of the timeless now.

This stillness is filled with goodness, with love and with wisdom.

This is what you are — always.

By grace you can now see your original face.

It is the face of your eternal soul.

Do not worry if some thoughts are still buzzing around.
By grace you remain as stillness.

Thoughts and feelings come and go.
Even the stars are coming and going.
The stillness of the sky stays.

You are that.
You are always that — vast and eternal.

Reiki is that — vast, eternal, filled with love, goodness, wisdom.

Consider yourselves as angels of light and love,
remaining temporarily on earth, while remembering source.

Can you hear wise crow, the messenger?
She connects you with source.

Source is wherever you are.

Love. Only love.
The miracle of love.

Reiki (4)

The light of Reiki is everywhere
and certainly where you are present.

After intense dedication, purification and meditation,
Dr. Mikao Usui received a precious gift for all of humanity.

The Reiki symbols came and descended
from a dimension of pure light and love.

Remember that you also have come from that dimension.

What comes from this dimension
can only find happiness by honoring light and love in life itself.

In Reiki you let the past heal.
You recognize the miracle of the present.
You welcome a bright future for all beings.

May the angels of Reiki inspire you and empower you.

In a world of chaos and injustice
Reiki creates a safe haven for peace, compassion and deep connection.

May Reiki be a channel for truth and wisdom.

Reiki (5)

To be a witness of the silence is to honor it.

Reiki is the intimate friend who comes knocking at your door
when the time has come for a deep change.

The initiation and the symbols received by Usui on the holy mountain
are being transmitted to you today in total respect of what you are.

The initiation is a package of concentrated love force
bundled in such a way that it speeds up your evolution
as a human and as a soul being.

The Reiki symbols are light and sound beings
traversing through all the imaginable dimensions.

During the initiation, light flows into matter
and creates a higher order.

Reiki (6)

After the grace of initiation
the ongoing discovery of what is new.
The strong invitation to let go of separation
and to allow connection.

This light, this magnificent light, is what you are.
Here you are at home.

The one who knows herself to be connected, heals.

The one who belongs to the immeasurable love of the cosmos
lives in peace and happiness.

Use the Reiki symbols as the diamond vehicle
to take you to the palace.

What you have come to claim here is your birthright.

The deepest wish of Reiki for you is that you may be at home, wherever you are.

Reiki (7)

There are so many wonderful ways of meditating.

Try them and choose the one that fits you.

It is always a good idea to surround yourself
with your beloved guides and teachers.

Today you could consider your meditation
as a timeless river of love and loving.

This river is always streaming strongly.

You can always, whenever you want, go and swim in that river.
Really!

Even when you feel separated from love,
it is always there for you.

Just be aware now —
loving and meditating belong to the same existential
category.

This is a great insight.

Your meditation and your introspection and your loving
are feeding the soul of the world.

Here your deep soul work and dream work are taking place,
sending love and Reiki for a better world.

Helping to manifest the next phase of human consciousness.
In the next stage, greed and the abuse of power and language
are being replaced by the delightful frequency of the heart.

Feel it.
Already the rhythm of the heart is here.

Here the limiting conditionings of the past are being healed
and your brain is being rewired.

All this takes place in the background as you are meditating.

In the midst of these evolutionary changes
there are many who experience fear.

Please be brave.

Keep witnessing the timeless river of loving.

Witnessing is a tremendous force of compassion.

Your loving presence is the healing.

Live in light, in love and in peace.

Planetary transformation

Go within. Go within.
What awaits you is the wonder of the eternal Self.
What a miracle; it is so near —
closer even than your heartbeat.

Once you are here,
you no longer feel like an animal on the chase.
You see through the confusion of illusion
into the clarity of truth.

Truth is not opposed to reality.
It welcomes what is.
It acts with wisdom.

It knows that violence begets more violence,
that only love is a radical response
to the woes in the world.

An eye for an eye does not lead anywhere.
Not in your own life.
Not in the life of nations.

To forgive is not to condone.
It is to establish the law of love
as the highest principle.

The Masters are working through you.
As they do, they purify your vehicle
and you are becoming more and more transparent.

In meditation you are holding space for planetary transformation.

Angel of the earth

The angel of the earth is here.
It is a very magnificent being.

Sometimes grace knocks on your door to deliver to you
a glimpse of the true reality, the authentic reality.

During such a glimpse of truth, your consciousness is so expanded
that you can perceive the goodness in all things.

During such a glimpse, you are no longer separated
from love, from beauty, from eternity.

You are no longer separated from the earth.
You feel her as an intelligent and living being.

You feel the heart of the earth beating in the cells of your own body.

It awakens such a deep sensitivity in you
that you become a citizen and a guardian of the earth.

As in the blessing ceremony of the Navajo people
you now walk in beauty on the earth.

You realize that beauty is before you, beauty is behind you, below you, above you and all around you.

Perceiving and caring for the beauty of the earth is a form of praying.

The angel of the earth is aware of your form of praying
and bestows upon you her magnificent energy.

As you resonate with the tone of the earth
your love becomes more grounded and more radiant.

Glory to you.
Glory to the earth.
Glory to all beings and all dimensions.

The angel of the earth is grateful to you.

One glimpse.
Just one glimpse of grace is sufficient.

True love knows no grievances

Straight from Source itself — receive the white and golden light of understanding.

True love knows no grievances.

Without grievances your experience is refreshing, childlike and full of wonder.

And... your life becomes much easier.

The New Age is already here for those who can see clearly, feel deeply and are willing to live from an open heart.

You can choose to live like this right now.

This decision and this choice are a very wise exercise of your free will.

No worries, no guilt, if you forget during the busyness of your life.
Choose again.

Every time you choose, you awaken
in the white and golden light of understanding.

In this way you are choosing for the well-being
of all your brothers and all your sisters wherever they may be.

Love is the highest vehicle for change.

Refusing to use hate to discriminate

Let the guides and angels of healing enter into your heart.

What is healing?

Meditating is healing.

Meditating is reaching beyond the obsessive thinker in your head.

Healing is seeing the difference between your limited self and the radiance of the true Self.

To affirm what you really are, you could say to yourself:
"I am limitless, effortless, pure awareness."

Limitless, effortless, pure awareness!

Loving is healing.

Trusting is healing.

Letting go is healing.

Speaking truth.

Taking responsibility ecologically, economically, politically.

Refusing to use hate to discriminate.

When you think of it, use your sweet mantra:
"I am limitless, effortless, pure awareness."

Or, "I am love. You are love. We are one."

Opening your heart, always opening your heart, is so healing.

Many millions of molecules in your body
are awakening in light and love, as your heart is opening.

You are the purity of radiant awareness.

You are.

Beyond the body.
Beyond the mind.
You always are.

The Now

Let your meditation be like water.

Running its course from source to the ocean.

Like the Tao, it brings you into harmony.

There is no goal.
Except to be and to be now.

And sharing your being and your loving where and when you can.

Lao Tzu says that the Tao is infinite, eternal.
Why is she eternal?
She is eternal because she is never born and therefore she cannot die.

This is true for you too.
Meditate on that.

Be that.
Now and always.

Powerful angels, compassionate bodhisattvas, immortal yogis
are all around you.

They are rejoicing with you the eternal truth of what you are.

No goal.
Just being.

No fear.
There is no dying of what you are.

In a split second the truth sets you free.

One liberation brings about ten more, and so on.

Nothing can stop you.
All rivers reach the ocean.

Now, you are closer than you have ever been.
This is the great joy of being in the Now.

The Tao also says...

Angels are always standing at your side.

Angels assist you with clarity, balance and perspective.

When injustice rules the land, they remind you that
nothing can stop you from experiencing the truth of what you are.

Forces of ignorance are dividing the people.

You are being invited to look at these seeming differences
and to come together in dialogue and healing
and to see the common ground.

Can you see now what never comes and goes
and lives forever in your awakened heart?

Love and truth are your common ground and your common
good.

From this space arises enlightened thinking,
enlightened speech and enlightened action.

In this space you can find a peace that cannot be disturbed
and a fire and a force for common good that can never be
extinguished.

The Tao says, Darkness gives birth to light.

The Tao also says, In darkness follow the authority of
Mother Nature
and stand in the middle, alone.

The goddess Athena, the goddess of justice, has owl as her
wisdom totem.

Owl is very happy to be with you as well.
Wisdom is just, is loving, is compassionate.

Trust in your wisdom to know what is true and what is not
true.

Ancient wisdom teachings of the mystery schools are as
valid as ever.

The central teaching is: Know thyself.

Or, as Jesus puts it in *A Course in Miracles*:
Teach only love, for that is what you are.

Shalom! Peace!

In the eye of the storm

In the eye of the storm, any storm — deep peace and quiet.

Can you be the still-point for a world in turmoil?

Can you be the angel and the prayer for protection
by being centered and surrendered?

You are sanctuary and place of refuge.

You are the love, the sweet love during and in between
your inbreath and your outbreath.

The mystic Meister Eckhart says,
The eye with which you see God,
is the same eye with which God is seeing you.

If you were a tree now,
your branches would be stretching and reaching
and bowing down to everyone in need of your support.

You are Jacob's ladder and angels are rushing up and down all the time.

You are the new consciousness and the new earth and a vehicle for healing.

The ones you have been waiting for are here now and you are aware of each other.

It is really everyone who can see through the single eye into the unity of all that is.

You have come for this.

One love.
One heart.
One people.

During the time of transformation there is both pressure and promise.

Each contribution has tremendous value.
Nothing is insignificant.

The next seven generations are already waiting in the wings.
Walk in peace.

You are uniting the world.

See the light.
See the light.

Seeking sincerely, earnestly, joyfully
and also being willing to find.

What are you finding?
The light of your true nature.

The love in your heart.

Your place on earth and in the cosmos.

Life beyond death.

Gratitude for what is — now, in this moment.

All this you are finding and much more
as you discover the truth of what you are.

Your fellow travelers are meeting you, wherever you are.

It is part of the divine plan and it requires your attention.

Sacred guides of love and light are pointing you in the right direction.

Even when you feel lost, the ones and the One,
who are looking out for you, are always here with you.
They do care, more than you can know.

All this is true from the vantage point of the realm of love,
where everything is always well.

Many humans and many countries have lost their direction.
This is the time for the great repair.

There is no better time for deep meditation.

The field you are generating, nourishes you and radiates out from you.

This field has no limitations.

Everything appears.

Everything disappears.
The field of love is.

You are.

No limitations.
No effort.
Just being.

This is life eternal.
This is life divine.

Such love you are.

Heart to heart.
Consciousness to consciousness.
You are uniting the world.

Keep the fire of awakening burning

Allow your breathing to become natural and peaceful.

Each time the love in your heart is meeting with the quiet in your mind,
you are receiving a beautiful benediction.

This you cannot force.

Just melt into it
by being open and receptive and knowing that this is your natural state.

Your natural state is to be relaxed presence and awareness.

It is legitimate to want to really experience your natural state.

It even makes total sense that you want this above anything else.

Claim the space in which you are in your natural state.

This eliminates your tendency to constantly lose yourself.

It is so exquisite to experience your natural state.

The love you are.

These blessed moments of relaxed presence and pure awareness
are allowing you to be taken back home.

Home is always where your heart is.

Here you are free to be.

Liberated from the attraction to distractions and detours,
life is so beautifully real and so very, very vibrant.

No moment in time is lost.

You are real.
Love is real.

Come home.
Here in this moment you belong.

The many lost souls on this planet
are finding a place of refuge in your awake heart.

This is your will and wish, supported by divine will.

Where there is a united will, there is a direct path.

You are the way and the light and the liberation.

Keep the fire of awakening burning.
It makes your heart very happy.

This is your precious earth

Many beings of light and love are here
to guide this meditation and transmission.

Start your meditation today with remembering
that your heart is powerful beyond imagination.

See your heart as a beautiful and large and mysterious crystal cave.

Enter the cave of your heart.
Keep walking as your eyes are adjusting to the darkness.

Sit down now and let your meditation deepen.

Invite light beings around you
as your heart is opening to its full capacity.

Yes.
Go deeper and deeper in your own being.

Release any and all limitations.

If fear to disappear arises, stay calm and alert and persist, remembering that your heart is the all-powerful and protecting and guiding force.

Listen to the words of Krishna spoken to Arjuna in the Bhagavad Gita:
"Even a little effort towards spiritual awareness
protects you from your greatest fear."

What is your greatest fear and at the same time your greatest longing?

Discovering what you really are — the eternal light in you.

The cosmic light in you, beyond the bounds of your personality.

The fear and the longing to discover your greatest talents and potential.

This is true for the individual and for the collective.

How to get there?
See the light.
See shadow.
Go beyond all dualities.

The world is full of it.
Fear and love.
Brutality and beauty.
Cold-hearted injustice and heartfelt justice.
Hate and compassion.

Your heart can hold all these dualities and transcend them.

Allow the cleansing through the element of water.

Embrace the truth of what you are.
Somehow it diminishes the suffering of all beings.

This is your precious earth.
It receives all your prayers.

Your loving presence on earth makes a big difference.

This sacred moment

Come with an open heart to this sacred moment.

Many divine mothers are meeting you here.

The opposite of unconscious dreaming is awakening.

Awakening is recognizing the innate perfection of what you have been
throughout eternity and also now, in this moment.

Awakening is celebrating the possibility of perfection in each moment.

This is your core practice — even when you do not feel 100% fine,
you are still 100% committed to fully being here and now.

This practice has a deep and beneficial effect on all of your life.

It fills your life with ease and acceptance
and it includes the joy of self-acceptance.

It fills your life with such a great sense of love and ongoing wonder.

You realize that your beloved ones are always with you.

You notice that your love is no longer limited to a dream of specialness.

Your loving and your awakening
have merged inside of you as one and the same.

Blame is gone.
Guilt is gone.
They have gone with the wind of change.

You are free now, totally free to be.

The divine mothers are sharing a loving and inclusive consciousness with you.

Receive this gift.

Receiving this gift, in the cells of your body, is helping to spread it around.

Can you see and feel this beautiful and almost unbearable light of your being?

This moment.
Always trusting what is present in this moment.

Sources

Preface

Duperly, Margaret. *Rainbow Earth Tarot.* (tarot cards and book)

Part I

Barthes, Roland. *Camera Lucida.*

Barthes, Roland. *Mythologies.*

Barthes, Roland. *Travels in China.*

Culler, Jonathan. *Barthes: A Very Short Introduction*

Jowett, George F. *The Drama of the Lost Disciples.*

Lavers, Annette. *Roland Barthes: Structuralism and After.*

Mann, Nicholas R. *The Isle of Avalon: Sacred Mysteries of Arthur and Glastonbury.*

Miller, D.A. *Bringing Out Roland Barthes.*

The Urantia Book.

Thody, Philip and Course, Ann. *Introducing Barthes*

Wheeler, Peter. *The Way of Love. Joseph of Arimathea Tells the True Story Behind the Message of Jesus.*

Part II

Eliade, Mircea. *Shamanism.*
Eliade, Mircea. *The Myth of the Eternal Return.*

Part III

Chapter 1

Brunton, Paul. *A Search in Secret India.*
Jacobs, Alan. *Ramana, Shankara and the Forty Verses.*
Maharshi, Ramana. *Talks with Ramana Maharshi,* Inner Directions Publishing
Maharshi, Ramana. *The Collected Works of Sri Ramana Maharshi,* Sri Ramanasramam
McMartin, Grace. *Absolute Consciousness.*
Natarajan, A.R. *Radiance of the Self.*
Natarajan, A.R. *Timeless in Time: Sri Ramana Maharshi*
Premananda (David, John), *Blueprints for Awakening.*
The Spiritual Teachings of Ramana Maharshi (with Foreword by C.G. Jung), Shambala Publications

Chapter 2

Campbell, Joseph. *The Hero's Journey: Joseph Campbell on His Life and Work.*
Campbell, Joseph and Moyers, Bill. *The Power of Myth.* (book and DVD)
Clottes, Jean. *La Grotte Chauvet: L'Art des Origines.*
Clottes, Jean and Lewis-Williams, David. *The Shamans of Prehistory. Trance and Magic in the Painted Caves.*
Curtis, Gregory. *The Cave Painters: Probing the Mysteries of the World's First Artists.*
Desondes, Flora. *Jóska Soós: The Shaman's Teaching.*
Garfield, Laeh Maggie. *Sound Medicine: Healing with Music, Voice and Song* (with a chapter on Jóska Soós)
Haich, Elisabeth. *Initiation.*

Harner, Michael. *Cave and Cosmos: Shamanic Encounters with another Reality.*
Herzog, Werner. *Cave of Forgotten Dreams.* (DVD, documentary)
Ingels, Tamara. *Jóska Soós: Shaman and Artist.*
Ingerman, Sandra. *Soul Retrieval: Mending the Fragmented Self.*
Ingerman, Sandra and Hank Wesselman. *Awakening to the Spirit World: The Shamanic Path of Direct Revelation.*
Moore, Robert and Gillette, Douglas. *The Magician Within: Accessing the Shaman in the Male Psyche.*
Narby, Jeremy and Huxley, Francis. *Shamans Through Time: 500 Years on the Path to Knowledge.*
Ryan, Robert E. *The Strong Eye of Shamanism: A Journey into the Caves of Consciousness.*
Tran, Christian. *Les Génies de la Grotte Chauvet.* (DVD, documentary)
Walsh, Roger. *The World of Shamanism: New Views of an Ancient Tradition.*
www.joskasoos.be

Chapter 3

Beckett, Don. *Reiki, The True Story: An Exploration of Usui Reiki*
Boräng, Kajsa Krishni. *Principles of Reiki.*
Brown, Fran. *Living Reiki: Takata's Teachings.*
Eos, Nancy. *Reiki and Medicine.*
Fueston, Robert N. *Reiki: Transmission of Light: Volume 1: The History and System of Usui Shiki Reiki Ryoho.*
Gray, John Harvey and Lourdes. *Hand to Hand: The Longest-Practicing Reiki Master Tells His Story*
Haberly, Helen J. *Reiki: Hawayo Takata's Story.*
Hammond, Sally. *We are all Healers.*
Hosak, Mark and Lübeck, Walter. *The Big Book of Reiki Symbols.*
Jonker, Jojan. *Reiki: The Transmigration of a Japanese Spiritual Healing Practice.*
Kelly, Maureen J. *Reiki and the Healing Buddha.*
Lugenbeel, Barbara Derrick. *Virginia Samdahl: Reiki Master Healer.*

Miles, Pamela. *Reiki: A Comprehensive Guide.*
Miller, Jessica A. *Reiki's Birthplace: A Guide to Kurama Mountain.*
Mitchell, Paul David. *Reiki: The Usui System of Natural Healing.* (The Blue Book)
Petter, Frank Arjava. *Reiki Fire: New Information about the Origins of the Reiki Power: A Complete Manual.*
Quest, Penelope. *Reiki for Life: The Complete Guide to Reiki Practice for Levels 1, 2 & 3.*
Stiene, Bronwen and Frans. *The Reiki Sourcebook.*
Twan, Anneli. *Early Days of Reiki: Memories of Hawayo Takata.*
Twan, Wanja. *In the Light of a Distant Star.*
Usui, Dr. Mikao and Petter, Frank Arjava. *The Original Reiki Handbook of Dr. Mikao Usui.*
https://reikiinmedicine.org (website of Pamela Miles)
www.reikialliance.com
www.reikitalkshow.com (nine years of interviews by Phyllis Lei Furumoto; also with Frank Coppieters on April 4th, 2013 and October 7th, 2014)
www.usuishikiryohoreiki.com

Chapter 4

Almaas, A.H. *Facets of Unity: The Enneagram of Holy Ideas.*
Anderson, Margaret. *The Unknowable Gurdjieff.*
Bennett, Elizabeth. *My Life, J.G. Bennett and G.I. Gurdjieff: A Memoir*
Bennett, J.G. *Enneagram Studies.*
Bennett, J.G. *Gurdjieff. A Very Great Enigma.*
Bennett, J.G. *How We Do Things: The Role of Attention in Spiritual Life.*
Bennett, J.G. *Transformation*
Bennett, J.G. *Witness: The Story of a Search*
Churton, Tobias. *Deconstructing Gurdjieff: Biography of a Spiritual Magician.*
Cristea, Alexandru Eugen. *Gurdjieff Movements.*
de Hartmann, Thomas and Olga. *Our Life with Mr. Gurdjieff.*
de Salzmann, Jeanne. *The Reality of Being: The Fourth Way of Gurdjieff.*

Gurdjieff, G.I. *Beelzebub's Tales to his Grandson: All and Everything: First Series*

Gurdjieff, G.I. *Meetings with Remarkable Men.*

Gurdjieff, G.I. *Views from the Real World.*

Korman, Mary Ellen. *A Woman's Work: The Spiritual Life Journey of Ethel Merston.*

Maitri, Sandra. *The Enneagram of Passions and Virtues: Finding the Way Home.*

Maitri, Sandra. *The Spiritual Dimension of the Enneagram: Nine Faces of the Soul.*

Moore, James. *Gurdjieff: A Biography.*

Needleman, Jacob (ed). *The Inner Journey: Views from the Gurdjieff Work.*

Nicoll, Maurice. *Psychological Commentaries on the Teaching of Gurdjieff and Ouspensky.*

Nicoll, Maurice. *The New Man: An Interpretation of Some Parables and Miracles of Christ.*

Nott, C.S. *Journey through this World: Meetings with Gurdjieff, Orage and Ouspensky.*

Nott, C.S. *Teachings of Gurdjieff: A Pupil's Journal.*

Ouspensky, P.D. *In Search of the Miraculous.*

Palmer, Helen. *The Enneagram: Understanding Yourself and Others in Your Life.*

Pentland, John. *Exchanges Within.*

Riso, Don Richard and Hudson, Russ. *The Wisdom of the Enneagram: The Complete Guide to Psychological and Spiritual Growth for the Nine Personality Types.*

Riso, Don Richard and Hudson, Russ. *Understanding the Enneagram: The Practical Guide to Personality Types.*

Rohr, Richard and Ebert, Andreas. *The Enneagram: A Christian Perspective.*

Shirley, John. *Gurdjieff: An Introduction to His Life and Ideas.*

Van Laer, Lee. *The Universal Enneagram.*

Meetings with Remarkable Men. Dir. Peter Brook. 1979. (film, DVD)

Chapter 5

Brook, Peter. The Empty Space.
Grotowski, Jerzy. Towards a Poor Theatre.
Richards, Thomas. At Work with Grotowski on Physical Actions.
Schechner, Richard and Wolford, Lisa. *The Grotowski Sourcebook.*

Chapter 6

Osho. *Courage: The Joy of Living Dangerously.*
Osho. *Creativity: Unleashing the Forces Within.*
Osho. *Emotions: Freedom from Anger, Jealousy and Fear.*
Osho. *Intimacy: Trusting Oneself and the Other.*
Osho. *Intuition: Knowing Beyond Logic.*
Osho. *Love, Freedom, Aloneness: The Koan of Relationships.*
Osho. *Tantra: The Supreme Understanding.*
Osho. *The Book of Secrets: 112 Meditations to Discover the Mystery Within.*
Osho. *Vedanta: Seven Steps to Samadhi.*
Punya, Yoga. *On the Edge: Living with an Enlightened Master.*
Subhuti, Anand. *My Dance with a Madman.*
Osho Zen Tarot. (tarot card deck and book)

Chapter 7

Chödrön, Pema. *Fail, Fail Again, Fail Better: Wise Advice for Leaning into the Unknown.*
Chödrön, Pema. *Taking the Leap: Freeing Ourselves from Old Habits and Fears.*
Chödrön, Pema. *The Places That Scare You: A Guide to Fearlessness in Difficult Times.*
Chödrön, Pema. *The Wisdom of No Escape: And the Path of Loving Kindness.*
Chödrön, Pema. *When Things Fall Apart: Heart Advice for Difficult Times.*

Trungpa, Chögyam and Gimian, Carolyn Rose(ed). *Ocean of Dharma: The Everyday Wisdom of Chögyam Trungpa.*
Hayward, Jeremy. *Sacred World: A Guide to Shambhala Warriorship in Daily Life.*
Hayward, Jeremy. *Warrior-King of Shambhala: Remembering Chögyam Trungpa.*
Midal, Fabrice. *Chögyam Trungpa: His Life and Vision.*
Midal, Fabrice(ed). *Recalling Chögyam Trungpa.*
Mukpo, Diana J. *Dragon Thunder: My Life with Chögyam Trungpa.*
Trungpa, Chögyam. *Cutting through Spiritual Materialism.*
Trungpa, Chögyam. *Milarepa.*
Trungpa, Chögyam. *Shambala: The Sacred Path of the Warrior.*
Trungpa, Chögyam. *The Lion's Roar: An Introduction to Tantra.*
Trungpa, Chögyam. *The Myth of Freedom and the Way of Meditation.*
Trungpa, Chögyam. *The Path Is the Goal: A Basic Handbook of Buddhist Meditation.*
Trungpa, Chögyam. *The Sanity We Are Born with: A Buddhist Approach to Psychology.*

Chapter 8

Dalal, A.S. *Eckhart Tolle & Sri Aurobindo: Two Perspectives on Enlightenment.*
Tolle, Eckhart. *A New Earth: Awakening to Your Life's Purpose.*
Tolle, Eckhart. *The Power of Now: A Guide to Spiritual Enlightenment.*
Tolle, Eckhart. *Stillness Speaks.*
Tolle, Eckhart. *The Power of Now: 52 Inspiration Cards.* (set of cards)

Chapter 9

Dr. Helen Schucman (scribe). *A Course in Miracles.*
Ferrini, Paul. *Reflections of the Christ Mind: the Present-Day Teachings of Jesus Christ.*
Harvey, Andrew. *Son of Man: The Mystical Path to Christ.*
Jesseph, Joe R. *A Primer of Psychology According to A Course in Miracles.*

Kisly, Lorraine(ed). *The Inner Journey: Views from the Christian Tradition.*

McCannon, Tricia. *Jesus: the Explosive Story of the Thirty Lost Years and the Ancient Mystery Religions.*

Miller, Patrick D. *Understanding A Course in Miracles.*

Strachan, Gordon. *Jesus the Master Builder: Druid Mysteries and the Dawn of Christianity.*

Wapnick, Kenneth. *Absence from Felicity: The Story of Helen Schucman and Her Scribing of A Course in Miracles.*

Wapnick, Kenneth. *Forgiveness and Jesus.*

Wapnick, Kenneth. *Journey through the Workbook of A Course in Miracles.*

Williamson, Marianne. *Return to Love: Reflections on the Principles of A Course in Miracles.*

Yogananda, Paramahansa. *The Second Coming of Christ: The Resurrection of the Christ Within You.*

Vahle, Neal. *A Course in Miracles: The Lives of Helen Schucman & William Thetford.*

Chapter 10

Aurobindo, Sri. *Sri Aurobindo On Himself.*

Aurobindo, Sri. *Savitri.*

Aurobindo, Sri. *The Integral Yoga.*

Aurobindo, Sri. *The Life Divine.*

Aurobindo, Sri. *The Mother.*

Aurobindo, Sri. *The Upanishads.*

Aurobindo, Sri and The Mother. *The Psychic Being (Soul: Its Nature, Mission, Evolution).*

Heehs, Peter. *The Lives of Sri Aurobindo.*

McDermott, Robert A (ed.). *The Essential Aurobindo: Writings of Sri Aurobindo.*

Mishra, Sampadananda. *Sanskrit: and the Evolution of Human Speech (Based on Sri Aurobindo's Linguistic Theory).*

Nirodbaran. *Twelve Years with Sri Aurobindo.*

Ramassamy, Dominique. *Un souffle venu de l'inde, Kiran Vyas, inspiré par Gandhi, Sri Aurobindo, et l'ayurvéda.*

Sarkar, Mona. *Douce Mère, Notes de Lumière.*

Satprem, *Mother or the Divine Materialism.*

Satprem. *Mother's Agenda (13 vols).*

Satprem. *Mother's Log: 1950-1973.*

Satprem. *The Mind of the Cells.*

Sethna, K.D. *The Mother: Past-Present-Future.*

The Mother. *Collected Works of the Mother: Words of The Mother.* Pub. Sri Aurobindo Ashram Publication Department.

Van Vreckhem, Georges. *Beyond the Human Species, The Life and Work of Sri Aurobindo and the Mother.*

Van Vreckhem, Georges. *Hitler and his God: The Background to the Nazi Phenomenon.*

Van Vreckhem, Georges. *The Mother: The Story of Her Life.*

Chapter 11

108: Mother Meera on Tour.

Linebaugh, Sonia L. *At the Feet of Mother Meera: The Lessons of Silence.*

Matousek, Mark. *Mother of the Unseen World: The Mystery of Mother Meera.*

Mother Meera. *Answers I.*

Mother Meera. *Answers II.*

Mother Meera. *Bringing Down the Light: Journey of a Soul after Death.*

Olati, Adilakshmi. *The Mother.*

Rüther, Sabine. *Children Experience Mother Meera: Divine Love from the Very Beginning.*

Chapter 12

Amritaswarupananda, Swami. *Ammachi: A Biography of Mata Amritanandamayi.*

Batchelder, Ram Das. *Rising in Love: My Wild and Crazy Ride to Here and Now with Amma, the Hugging Saint.*

Bess, Savitri L. *The Path of the Mother: With the Divine Guidance of the Holy Mother Amma.*

Dayalu (Zeff, Ted), *AMMA: Inspiring Experiences with the Divine Mother.*

Halpern, Jake. "Amma's Multifaceted Empire, Built on Hugs." *The New York Times* May 25, 2013.

Hixon, Lex. *Great Swan: Meetings with Ramakrishna.*

Puri, Swami Paramatmananda. *Dust of Her Feet: On Amma's Teachings, Vol.1.*

Walker III, Ethan. *A Pilgrim's Guide to Amma.*

Darshan: The Embrace. Dir. Jan Kounen. 2005. (DVD, documentary)

Un + une. Dir. Claude Lelouch. 2015. (film in which Amma gives darshan at the end)

Part IV

Fox, Matthew & Rupert Sheldrake. *The Physics of Angels: Exploring the Realm Where Science and Spirit Meet.*

Graham, Ian with White Bull. *God Is Never Late...But Never Early Either! Reassurance for Humanity from Another Dimension.*

Mallasz, Gitta & Fischli, Lela. *Talking with Angels. Budaliget 1943.*

Shourie, Arun. *Two Saints: Speculations Around and About Ramakrishna Paramahamsa and Ramana Maharshi.*

Wohlleben, Peter. *The Hidden Life of Trees: What They Feel, How They Communicate.*

Made in the USA
Middletown, DE
23 August 2019